What to Do in Case of a Choir Rehearsal

James D. Woodward

Illustrated by
Wm. James Brown

CHURCH STREET PRESS

© Copyright 1972 • Convention Press
All rights reserved
Nashville, Tennessee
5167-08

Dewey Decimal Classification: 783.8
Printed in the United States of America

Contents

Introduction ix
1. PLANNING AND SCHEDULING 3
2. THE EFFICIENT REHEARSAL 17
3. WHAT TO TEACH ABOUT BREATHING 27
4. WHAT TO TEACH ABOUT VOWELS AND CONSONANTS 37
5. CONDUCTING 51
6. INTERPRETATION 73
7. THE DIRECTOR AS LEADER 87
8. THE DIRECTOR AS TEACHER TO THE CONGREGATION 97
9. CONTINUING PREPARATION 107
Personal Learning Activities 109

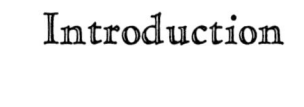

Introduction

On an occasion of this kind it becomes more than a moral duty to speak one's mind; it becomes a pleasure.

OSCAR WILDE, 1856–1900

Introduction

YOUTH AND ADULT CHOIR MEMBERS come in a variety of sizes, shapes, temperaments, and "musical smart." Their motivations for participating may be spiritual, musical, social, or a combination thereof. The choir director's task is to confront these varied personalities, backgrounds, and motivations with rehearsal and performance experiences that are meaningful and satisfying to all. What an intimidating task!

This book is an effort to provide suggestions for accomplishing that task. It is aimed primarily at the nonprofessional director, but hopefully it will remind the most experienced of us of some things we know to do but perhaps haven't been doing adequately. A "mini-book" like this is obviously not an attempt to discuss in detail the mysteries of the various technical subjects raised. Most of these subjects have been explored innumerable times in print already, and by far more gifted and experienced writers and musicians than I.

It is hoped, instead, that this little volume can serve as a practical handbook for dealing on a limited basis with the prob-

The choir member comes in a variety of sizes, shapes and temperaments

lems so common to all volunteer choirs and directors. Even an "old pro" may find himself reflected in these pages now and then, for they represent not so much the wisdom I have accumulated as the mistakes I have made. Like Thomas Edison's, much of my progress lies in having discarded hundreds of things that did not work.

If any of these suggestions will work for you, then I'll be delighted. If not, be of good cheer. The book doesn't really cost very much.

1. Planning and Scheduling

He flung himself upon his horse and rode madly off in all directions.

STEPHEN LEACOCK, 1869–1944

1. Planning and Scheduling

IT SEEMS all too obvious to say that the leader must be thoroughly prepared before the rehearsal; yet many rehearsals are filled with wasted time because of a common shortcoming—insufficient preparation. The director must know which songs he is going to rehearse, what he hopes ultimately to accomplish with each, and what he must accomplish with each in that particular rehearsal. Since the question of which songs (or how many) is more properly related to long-range planning, let's defer that discussion and deal now with the last two areas.

The director's most demanding responsibility is that of stewardship of rehearsal time. How often have we argued the merits of spending that time learning music *versus* learning *about* music? Some directors lament their choir's rote-learning process and claim there is never time left after the note pounding to deal with music reading or interpretation, much less their choral sound! Others lecture profoundly and at such length on their literature that the singers end up very knowledgeable about everything except the notes they are expected to sing next Sunday. What, then, should our approach be?

The ideal director should be both a dash
and a distance man

It would seem that the ideal director should be both a "dash" and a "distance" man. That is, his rehearsals should be efficient and economical, with adequate attention to learning the notes (doesn't Sunday come three times a week?) and at the same time be a progressive learning experience that has a cumulative effect on the participants. So let's begin with a consideration of ways we might use the time available to us.

I have long felt that among its other attributes, heaven would be a place of unlimited rehearsal time. It doesn't seem to matter whether we rehearse an hour after prayer meeting or five days a week, there is just never as much time as we think we need. Whatever time is available to us, then, is precious, and must be utilized accordingly. Let's begin by considering two kinds of rehearsal planning: the individual rehearsal (the dash) and the long-range preparation (the distance). We'll start with a look at the long view.

If we look closely at our teaching methods, we may find that our greatest shortcoming lies in inadequate long-range scheduling. (By "long range," I mean planning music from three to twelve months in advance.) It directly influences the teaching of music *per se* and the teaching *about* music so essential to the building of a good choir. Let me describe the way it is often done, then suggest some ways that might be better.

The director in question (hereafter known as "Hero") is a very busy man. So busy in fact, that he has not given any thought to choir rehearsal. Consequently, he arrives early—ten minutes—in order to "prepare." There are two numbers in the folders. One is last Sunday's anthem and the other totals only seven copies. (He had meant to reorder.) What to do for Sunday? Hero feverishly flips through his file. Here's anthem "A" . . . too hard. What about anthem "B"? . . . The pastor doesn't like it . . . not evangelistic enough. Anthem "C" . . . great idea! . . . Uh-oh, not enough copies, so forget it. [He'd have to reorder that one, too, sometime.] Anthem "D" . . . did it five weeks ago, but nobody will remember, so get it out. Anthem "E"... don't know this one, but it looks OK. Anthem "F"... here's a good one, and we haven't done it in a couple of years. Anthem "G"... eight parts, but it'll do. Pull it, and let's go.

Hero now has four tunes to rehearse. He madly deals out the music and is finally ready to start... only ten minutes late. It's OK, though. No one expected to start on time, and choir members are still arriving. The crowd's kind of small, so we'll give them five more minutes.

Rehearsal finally begins. Hero starts with anthem "D," and announces that it is for Sunday morning. A chorus of groans wells up. They have sung it four times this year... they did it last month... they're tired of it... they don't want to do it Sunday. Anything to keep the troops happy. Our Hero retreats, and anthem "D" is passed in. Hero begins to get that crowded feeling. Anthem "F" now seems the most likely possibility for Sunday. After all, didn't they do it two years ago? They sing it through. A third of his choir has joined since it was sung last. They are sight-reading, and the others seem to have forgotten that one night they rehearsed it for nearly an hour. The evening settles down to a valiant attempt to whip anthem "F" into shape for Sunday. Forty-five minutes later they are able to sing straight through without its falling apart, even though the bass singers swear they will never make it, and two altos declare they will not come on Sunday and be embarrassed. Nevertheless, Hero has triumphed again, and another Sunday is "prepared."

Time for a break and business meeting. Twenty minutes are consumed while choir members discuss details for a party to be scheduled sometime next month, and all the would-be comedians get in their licks. Now, only ten minutes are left, so *der big schtick* calls for anthem "G," the eight-part one. They struggle through it while our resident genius attempts to cover,

The director, hereafter known as Hero . . .

then balance all the parts with his smallish choir . . . no way. "Turn it in, folks. We'll save this one till the absentees are all here." Two minutes left; might as well try that new one, anthem "E." Much harder than it looked. What does the composer mean by all those meter changes? How was I to know the organist couldn't sight-read it? "We're just too tired; let's call it a night. Thank you, Lord, for bringing us together to sing your praises . . . Everybody be here Sunday. Section leaders, call those absentees."

The next Wednesday, 7:20 P.M., Hero arrives early. There are two anthems in the folders . . . last Sunday's (what a disaster!) and that tough one he didn't know how to conduct. Hero feverishly flips through the file . . .

Everyone of us has been guilty of some, and probably all, of Hero's transgressions. Our mythical friend is slowly killing off a good choir, not because he is a poor musician or a bad guy, but simply because he never thinks more than four days ahead. If we are really serious about doing some meaningful teaching, we must plan carefully *before* we reach the classroom.

The Anthem Schedule

The most important time the director spends is that given to planning his anthem schedule. The busier he is (part-time), the more desperate his need to set aside an hour or so periodically to block out his literature schedule. I prefer a quarterly anthem schedule, with significant dates beyond that quarter (special programs, revivals, retreats, banquets, etc.) noted at the end. Some directors plan much further ahead, which is fine as long as their schedules remain realistic and workable. A shorter time ceases to qualify as long range.

Before beginning to plan, the director must have all the pertinent dates that affect him and the group (youth or adult) at his disposal. He needs his personal calendar, the church calendar, the associational and state calendars, and possibly the public-school calendar. (Watch those football weekends and holidays.) A good way to start is by collecting pertinent dates from the various calendars and noting them on your personal calendar or a separate calendar set aside for this purpose.

The choice of an anthem for a given Sunday will be influenced by a variety of things. We talk a good deal about choosing music to go with the sermon. This sounds better than it works. It is the rare pastor who knows what he is going to preach one month ahead, much less than months in advance. If we are trying to work five to eight weeks ahead (the object of the whole discussion), there is little we can do to coordinate anthem and sermon. Just do your best planning, let the pastor know you will be glad to prepare anything he likes with X numbers of weeks' notice, and don't worry about it. Of course, if you *have* a pastor who schedules well ahead, take advantage of the suggestions his subjects will offer. His subjects make your job easier and contribute to some beautiful worship services. Actually, the factors contributing to your choices are not likely to be aesthetic ones. Here are some things to think about when scheduling:

1. Special emphases
2. Holiday weekends
3. Special programs (concerts)
4. Vacation months
5. Seasonal emphases
6. Absence of director or organist

You can add your own items to this list, but the point is obvious. No intelligent director plans a big, eight-part anthem for Labor Day weekend or during those worst summer weekends. It is not smart to give a substitute organist or director a really thorny number; neither is it wise to plan a string of difficult anthems concurrently with the preparation of a major work (special program).

Once you have ascertained these influences, it is fairly easy to take advantage of the suggestions they offer and avoid the problems they present. Make out the schedule (do any necessary reordering *then*), duplicate it so the choir can have individual copies in each folder, and post one on the bulletin board. Naturally there will be occasional changes. Just don't make so many that you destroy the integrity of the schedule. If that becomes necessary, then the planning wasn't really very good to start with.

The Rehearsal Schedule

A frequently asked question is: "How many anthems should I try to rehearse each week?" The answer is dictated by the rehearsal time available. If the rehearsal is one hour long, try to cover five anthems. If you have two hours, eight tunes make a reasonable goal. Of course, six or seven can be worked for rehearsal lengths in between. To many readers, these numbers may seem a bit high; but it has been my observation that most of us spend too much time on too few anthems. A number that has been rehearsed ten minutes a week for six weeks will be better prepared than one that receives twenty minutes a week for three weeks, even though they both get sixty minutes of rehearsal. The longer exposure in smaller doses is a better teaching process. Besides, the penalty to the absentee is not nearly so great. By missing one rehearsal, he loses only one sixth of the time devoted to a particular number rather than one third. I am not suggesting that rehearsal time be divided equally among the anthems, but merely pointing out that the more frequently the choir members are exposed to the music, the better they will learn it.

When we have determined how many numbers we can cover, we are ready to plan the rehearsal itself. We refer to the long-range schedule to see what is on for the next X number of weeks. If we decide we can work six anthems per rehearsal, then obviously we will be working six weeks ahead.

It is difficult, if not undesirable, to rigidly assign time blocks to each anthem; but certain principles can serve us well. Here are some:

1. Begin with familiar material that is not vocally demanding. This is especially important if warm-ups or other vocalises are not used, for it gives the latecomers time to get settled, and the voices a chance to warm.

2. Get right to the hardest or most intense work of the evening. The first hour of a rehearsal is usually the most productive. After that, the efficiency curve begins to plummet. This block of time should include next Sunday's anthem, new material, and the "woodshedding" and nit picking necessary to thorough rehearsal.

3. Taper off toward the end. Have the big anthems and difficult passages behind you. Look again for familiar material that is easy on the voice and brain (a good spot for responses, new hymns, etc.).

A word about Sunday's anthem—work it early, but *after* everyone is there. If you have worked your schedule well, it should not require much rehearsal. If it should disintegrate in your hands, and you have to spend thirty minutes putting it back together, you will at least have time to do so—but you are in trouble. Your rehearsal plan is shot, and the anthem schedule is in jeopardy.

Always take a hard look at the anthem scheduled for a week from Sunday. That's the time to determine whether it is maturing on schedule and can be polished up in ten or fifteen minutes the following week. If you decide it cannot, then adjust your rehearsal plan accordingly, *or* swap places with a tune on the schedule that *can* be made ready next week. A good guideline is this one: The choir should be able to sing two anthems on any given Sunday—the one scheduled and the one planned for the following week. If you follow this rule, you and your choir are *never* poorly prepared and insecure on Sunday. And by the way, teacher, be sure to explain the significance of *next* week's anthem to the choir. Then they can keep track of their personal progress more accurately. (Wouldn't it be marvelous to have them sweating over the anthem scheduled ten days away?)

The most carefully planned rehearsal and anthem schedule can be wiped out with the addition of a cantata or choir program. How can we possibly include the preparation of a major work in this already tightly structured time? Here are two suggestions:

1. PLAN THE PROGRAM WELL AHEAD. Decide on the work and get the music on hand. Start it early enough to avoid the last-minute panic. The director who is madly trying to schedule an eleventh-hour rehearsal on the cantata is a man who has misjudged the amount of work involved in preparing it. What a disservice we have done to our choir members when they approach a performance with dread and insecurity instead of excited expectancy. Why punish ourselves with these programs if they are not happy, gratifying experiences? None of us is so naïve that we don't know that these extra programs will require extra rehearsals. When you schedule the performance, also schedule whatever extra rehearsals you feel will be necessary. (I call them *bonus* rehearsals.) Discus these with the choir members in order to determine the most convenient times. Once *they* have chosen the dates, put them on the printed anthem schedule. That way, when the time arrives, members can hardly claim prior commitments.

Bonus rehearsals are most fruitful, I believe, when used at the beginning of the preparation rather than near the performance date. That way, the initial exposure to the music is massive and forceful rather than the "picking around the edges" that the regular rehearsal provides. The choir will get deeply involved much earlier with this approach. Also, this is the ideal time for sectional rehearsals, which I believe can be used to maximum advantage *at the beginning.* If you are having sectionals the week before D day, in a last-ditch effort to learn the notes, you are in bad trouble.

Also, if the major portion of the learning is done early, the work can *soak* longer and can be polished at a more leisurely pace. This results in maximum security for the singers and a high degree of "finish" for the music.

2. IN ADDITION TO THE BONUS REHEARSALS, we will want to apply a portion of our weekly rehearsal time to the cantata. That means hollowing out a place for it in the rehearsal plan. It would seem wise to forego the joys of long and complicated anthems for a season—at least very many of them. Choose music in that quarter that can be prepared with a minimum of effort. This would also be an excellent time to repeat a favorite or two.

There is nothing wrong with judicious repetition. Favorites that we particularly enjoy and a new anthem (especially if it's contemporary in style) can profit from a relatively early second hearing. The principle here is that we repeat specifically and by design, and not because we are desperate for a "sugar-stick" for Sunday.

Together, these two adjustments will permit you to drop one or two anthems from the rehearsal plan (you won't need to work quite so far ahead) or spend a bit less time on each anthem, or both. Just make absolutely certain that the quality of your Sunday work doesn't deteriorate. We've all known directors whose special programs were well done, with everything in between sounding like an afterthought.

Incidentally, after the cantata has been under rehearsal for a while, choruses can be used effectively in the Sunday worship services. This enables us to get double mileage from the time spent preparing them. There are other advantages, too. The choir gets an extra performance under its belt, and the congregation gets a preview of the cantata to come, both excellent fringe benefits. Study the cantata with this goal in mind when making the anthem schedule around it.

2. The Efficient Rehearsal

Genius is one per cent inspiration and ninety-nine per cent perspiration.

THOMAS ALVA EDISON, 1847–1931

2. The Efficient Rehearsal

ALL THE PLANNING in the world will not compensate for poor rehearsal techniques. It is possible to plan conscientiously and well, then fail to translate those plans into good choral work because we fail to rehearse efficiently. Let's run a quick inventory of good rehearsal habits.

When we bring our plans to rehearsal, we should have a fair idea of what we need to accomplish with each anthem in that rehearsal. One may require only a reading by way of introduction. Another may require attention to a section, a page, or perhaps just a passage. The important thing is that we know what needs work, and then get to it. A common error is aimless reading of the material. "That's pretty good; let's do it again." Three minutes later, "That's better; let's try it again. This time, put something in it." Three minutes later, after "something" has been added, "That's a lot better. Now, once more from the top." What a colossal waste of time! Sure, there's some benefit in reading the music three times, but how much more efficient to isolate the bad spots and devote the time to correcting them, rather than dissipating it on the pages that present no problems.

Obviously, everything cannot be fixed at once. The experienced conductor knows what to correct now and what to defer to a later rehearsal. Ultimately, however, he must deal with everything he wants changed. Problems rarely correct themselves, and the leader who shrugs and thinks maybe it will be all right is deluding himself. Years ago I read a sign in a choir room that went something like this: "Nothing good ever happens in the choir loft that hasn't already happened in the rehearsal room. Nor does anything bad." This little slogan carries a mountain of truth and can virtually revolutionize one's rehearsal habits. It is saying simply that what we want to hear in the sanctuary must first be accomplished in the choir room. That is fairly obvious. Few of us expect a mediocre choir to assume greatness just by walking into the loft. It's the second sentence that haunts us. It is suggesting that all the little bad sounds we heard Sunday had actually been around for several weeks. We either tolerated them, didn't notice them, or didn't care. If your position is either (or both) of the last two, you ought seriously to consider another line of work. But what about tolerating sounds we know to be bad? Isn't that just as deplorable? I'm glad you asked that question, sir, for it leads me to the next point.

The average Youth or Adult choir is made up of average people with average skills. It will rehearse from one to two hours a week; and, though capable of beautiful work, it will not likely achieve perfection under those circumstances. The sobering conclusion, then, is that we must change the things we can, *tolerate* the things we can't change, and have the sense to know the difference (you may quote me). In effect, every anthem is a compromise—a bitter word for us artists, but the right one nevertheless. Don't misunderstand. This realization is not an instant license for sloppy work or limited goals. We are still committed to do the best that is in us. We are just admitting that we can't get it all done, and therefore must decide what we will do. This means rehearsal priorities.

Undoubtedly there are almost as many concepts of priorities as there are directors, and you must decide what is most important to you. I will list my own in the hope that they will stimulate you to think through yours.

PITCHES AND RHYTHMS—Absolutely fundamental to the learning procedure is a mastery of the basic musical mechanics: melodies, harmonies, and rhythms. In my judgment, there is little point in getting involved with the more subtle aspects until this foundation is laid. Learn the notes, tune the chords, and make the rhythms, including attacks and releases, precise. (*Everybody* notices if we don't start and stop together!) You may not be making music at this point, but you will certainly be ready to *begin* making music.

There are those who feel that a preoccupation with mechanical accuracy makes for detached, cerebral singing. They would be less concerned with such trivia and concentrate instead on singing "from the heart." No one is opposed to music coming from the heart. That would be comparable to being against motherhood and the flag in our business. It's just that no amount of heart, sincerity, or anguished facial expressions can compensate for bad intonation, erratic rhythms and tempos, and a careless approach to attacks and releases. Robert Shaw is quoted as saying, "God loves right notes." I believe he does, and I'm with him. That's why I think the place to begin is by mastering the printed page.

DYNAMICS AND INTERPRETATION—I'll use these two words to represent a variety of areas. Actually, we're still talking about the printed page, but now in its more subtle aspects. It is in this stage that we shape phrases, smooth *crescendos* and *decrescendos*, perfect the *sforzando* or *subito piano*, and in general cope with the more sophisticated musical devices. At this point I would concentrate on the meaning and message of the anthem, pointing out how the musical devices serve to underscore and highlight. By this time, choir members must have no doubt about what the text is saying, and will be concentrating on unmistakably communicating it.

TONE AND DICTION—Like love and marriage, it's difficult to discuss one of these without the other. The vowels will need constant attention. After all, our charges spend their waking hours talking like Southerners, or Westerners, or Easterners, and then are expected to speak "English" for the choir. It's no wonder that they need a bit of prompting. Remind them of the desired colors and reassert the unification. Remember, as the vowel goes, so goes the tone.

The consonants may well have been covered already, under phase one or two. But if any words lack clarity, precision, or dramatic content, some additional reminding at this point can provide that final luster.

The astute reader has probably already muttered to himself, "But you can't separate or compartmentalize these areas," and indeed he is largely correct. Most of us attempt to work in two or more of these areas or phases as we go along, simply because efficiency is better served and the teaching more graphically demonstrated. If we know from the outset that we are going to be able to accomplish everything we desire for the music, these priorities need not concern us. We can even perfect everything in every phrase as we go along if we choose. Perhaps such a situation exists, but I've never encountered it.

What I'm trying to say can be illustrated with this experience. A workshop chorus had a week to prepare and perform a well-known oratorio. The conductor worked long and in minute detail on the first few choruses. We all marveled at the extent of his knowledge and his desire for perfection, but the week slipped away before those attributes were applied to the latter part of the work. During the performance, the first part was marvelously performed. The last part was a shambles. Our conductor had devoted much of his limited rehearsal time to "finishing" the house before he had laid all the foundation. This can be done with a single three-minute hymn arrangement as easily as with a two-hour oratorio. We must decide what we *must* do in contrast to what we would like to do. Accomplish the first, get as far along on the second as humanly possible, and then tolerate, albeit unwillingly, what remains undone. In short, *plan the rehearsal.*

One last suggestion toward efficient rehearsing. Have pencils available and see that they are used. This will require each choir member's having the same music every week, a simple feat accomplished with some kind of inexpensive rehearsal folder and enough music to go around. Put pencils in the folders, and keep spares available. Encourage the singers to use them liberally (and lightly) at their own discretion in addition to any marks you might suggest. Choir members tend to think they will remember your instructions and directions. They won't. The same points will have to be made over and over—a foolish and boring waste of time that could be easily avoided with a few pencil marks. Choir members reach a degree of polish in proportion to the number of times they have to be told the same things. In other words, a director could make fifty separate suggestions about a piece of music, or he could use the same amount of time making ten suggestions, five different times. If your choir members make mistakes, give them pencils. If you ever make mistakes, see that they have erasers!

On Singing from Memory

The subject of memory work by church groups is frequently discussed and is of increasing interest among directors everywhere. The questions range from "How do you get them to do it?" to "What's the point in doing it at all?" Since memorizing is a direct result of the teaching techniques employed, it may be helpful to discuss the practice, with its pros and cons.

The greatest single advantage to singing from memory is the undivided attention given the director. The heightened rapport that automatically results from such attention is obvious in the sound. This is especially true if the director in turn gives all, or most, of his attention to the choir as opposed to his music. There are other advantages, such as appearance, dramatic impact, and showmanship; but these pale beside the one great asset.

There is also a disadvantage, and that is the time required to memorize past the point where the anthem is thoroughly learned and could be competently performed. The director who wants his choir to perform from memory must determine how much additional time is required and then weigh the expenditure of that time against the advantage gained before making his decision. If he should decide to try it, there are some other things he should bear in mind.

Singing from memory should not be an end in itself. It is quite possible to so concentrate your efforts on memorizing notes and words that the more subtle aspects of the music go begging. Instead, it should be a by-product of long-range planning and thorough rehearsal. Most anthems that are carefully worked for five, six, or seven weeks would be very nearly memorized by many choir members anyway. Very likely there would be no additional time needed. This is especially true if a choir member realizes from the moment he sees a piece of music that ultimately it must be memorized. From the first reading, his whole attitude toward the anthem is different.

Choir members who are singing without music in their hands are more dependent on the conductor. That is both good and bad. It means they will be sensitive to his every twitch, but it also means that he must throw cues and releases more frequently and consistently.

Singing from memory solves the problem of the Sunday morning choir member. No one in his right mind would drop in to sing "memorized music" on Sunday if he had not been to several rehearsals. In fact, the whole idea of memory work is a great morale builder for most choir members. They attend better, work harder, and take a healthy pride in the organization. These are all valid goals and adequately answer the questions about why we should do it. The question of how to start is a little tougher.

Many choirs ease into memory work gradually. They may decide to memorize one anthem a month or to sing any repeated anthem without music. After recovering from the first traumatic shock, most groups are enthusiastic and eager to try again. It is important that the first attempts be successful and pleasant. For that reason, the first selections should not be too complex, and should be music the choir has lived with for a while.

In presenting the idea to a choir (the officers can be of help here), it may be wise to suggest a trial period of one or two months. Either the choir members will discover that they are perfectly capable of memory work on a continuing basis, or the director will realize that an occasional effort would be more practical for his group.

Several factors determine a choir's ability to sing from memory, among them the amount of rehearsal time, the musical background of the choir members, and the skill of the director, both as teacher and conductor. Not all choirs should attempt to sing everything from memory, but all choirs would profit from the experience as often as it is practicable.

3. What to Teach About Breathing

Habit is habit, and not to be flung out of the window by any man, but coaxed downstairs a step at a time.

                    MARK TWAIN, 1835–1910

3. What to Teach About Breathing

VIRTUALLY EVERY BOOK on singing has a chapter on breathing. It's usually at or near the front, and for obvious reasons. It is the foundation of all singing. Until good breath support is mastered, any singing, individual or collective, is severely limited. It is not my purpose here to attempt a comprehensive discussion of breathing. There is an abundance of excellent books on the subject, and the person who wishes detailed information will have no trouble finding it. I would like to describe the basic process and mention some ways it might be taught within the context of a rehearsal. Thus far, I have made no distinction between the teaching techniques for adult and youth, nor will I now. I will, however, approach this subject with the teen-ager specifically in mind; not because the problem is peculiar to that age, but because it seems to be more limiting and difficult to deal with the adolescent. Besides, if you can teach it to teens, you can certainly get it across to adults.

Proper breathing is effected when the abdominal area is allowed to expand (all the way around) and the rib cage is held high and fairly stationary. The feeling is that of pulling the air deep into the body rather than into the chest. There are two great advantages to the singer: (1) his air capacity is greater; and (2) the emission, or spending of air, is subject to much more positive control.

It's difficult to say why teen-agers are such notorious "backward" (chest) breathers, but the fact is reflected in the thin, breathy sound that is the trademark of the Youth choir. Some writers believe it is because of the figure consciousness that comes with adolescence. What self-respecting young man or woman would be caught dead with the abdomen protruding? Whatever the cause, the cure must be effected before any singing of consequence can be accomplished.

The task is to discover and experience the role of the body in singing. The average teen-ager sings from the neck up. The air is spent by allowing the chest to collapse gradually on the lungs, squeezing it out like toothpaste from a tube. We must help the singers grasp the concept of the high chest and lots of lung room, with the muscles around the middle controlling the flow of air. These additional devices may help.

To demonstrate what proper breathing looks like, ask a volunteer to lie down on the floor or on a pair of piano benches. Point out that when we are prone or asleep, Mother Nature takes over, and we breathe correctly without working at it. Place two or three books on the "victim's" abdomen. The hard surface on which the victim lies will flatten the shoulder blades and raise the rib cage. The books will rise and fall while the chest remains still. Now choir members know what the process looks like, and can experience it themselves with a little floor space and a good book. Of course, when they stand up, they will go back to the old way; but at least they are aware of what they are looking for.

Since it is impractical to stretch an entire choir out on the floor, we need another approach for practice *en masse*. Have

... the abdominal area is allowed to expand

the singers clasp their hands behind their heads and spread their elbows. Again we've managed to raise the rib cage, which is always step 1. Then see how completely they can inhale and exhale without moving the chest and shoulders. There is only one area left to move; and often the light will dawn with this simple gimmick.

If they are still not convinced that it is really nature's way, ask them to observe the breathing of a child, the smaller the better. Children, especially little babies, haven't yet learned to do it wrong. Everything works just as it was intended, and this may encourage our would-be singers to abandon their wrong breathing habits.

If you have a doctor in your choir or church, ask him to explain the anatomy involved in the breathing process. Often a simple diagram on the chalkboard will clear up many misconceptions and speed up the learning process. Such a diagram is very interesting, and choir members of all ages are usually fascinated with it.

Incidentally, we can make that figure-consciousness mentioned earlier work for us rather than against us. Explain that correct breathing in general, and particularly in singing, is a great muscle conditioner, and will contribute to a flat, hard midsection. (Who among us doesn't want that?) Speak a good deal about the strength and muscle required for singing. Challenge some of the athletes to a phrase-sustaining contest (provided you're sure you can win). In every way possible, picture breath and body control as attractive and desirable skills. Once they acquire them, they can learn to sing.

Long after our singers have begun to breathe correctly, they will be struggling to apply the breath correctly. The former is much easier to teach and learn than the latter.

An invaluable aid to correct breath application is the *staccato* exercise. The diaphragm goes wild on a well executed *staccato* note or scale, and the sensation produced is quite vivid. Also point out the laughing process. All of us use the diaphragm then, and that can help nail down the concept.

Sometime during a rehearsal, have the singers stand, put their palms together in front of their chests, and press hard as they sustain a phrase, *crescendo,* or go for a high note. This isometric approach to involving the body muscles in support of the voice has special appeal for the boys.

We should understand by now that the problem is not so much in developing new energy sources, but in harnessing those we use routinely in countless other ways. It's not an easy thing to do, and will require all the ingenuity you can muster. The rewards are great, however, and well worth the time and effort for everyone concerned.

The first step toward applying that newly developed deep breathing may lie in our getting over our fear of damaging the "delicate" little singing instrument. Please hear me out before you burn the book. The instrument *is* delicate, and we must certainly deal with it with care and respect; but we must not forever tiptoe around it, afraid to demand a solid, "gutsy" *fortissimo.*

Have you ever watched and listened to your choir members at a football game? The noise is deafening and its authors indefatigable; yet they rarely lose their voices, even in the night air. How can they produce such vigorous, penetrating sound under those circumstances and sound so pathetic in choir rehearsal? Evidently it's because they shout better, or if you please, more correctly, than they sing. The trick, then, is to help them make the transfer from one to the other, from the known to the unknown.

In its simplest form, singing is nothing more than sustained speech. Loud singing, then, is loud speech, or to put it another way, a controlled shout. Since they already have the shouting down, all we need to do is concentrate on the application of the breath that will result in the necessary control.

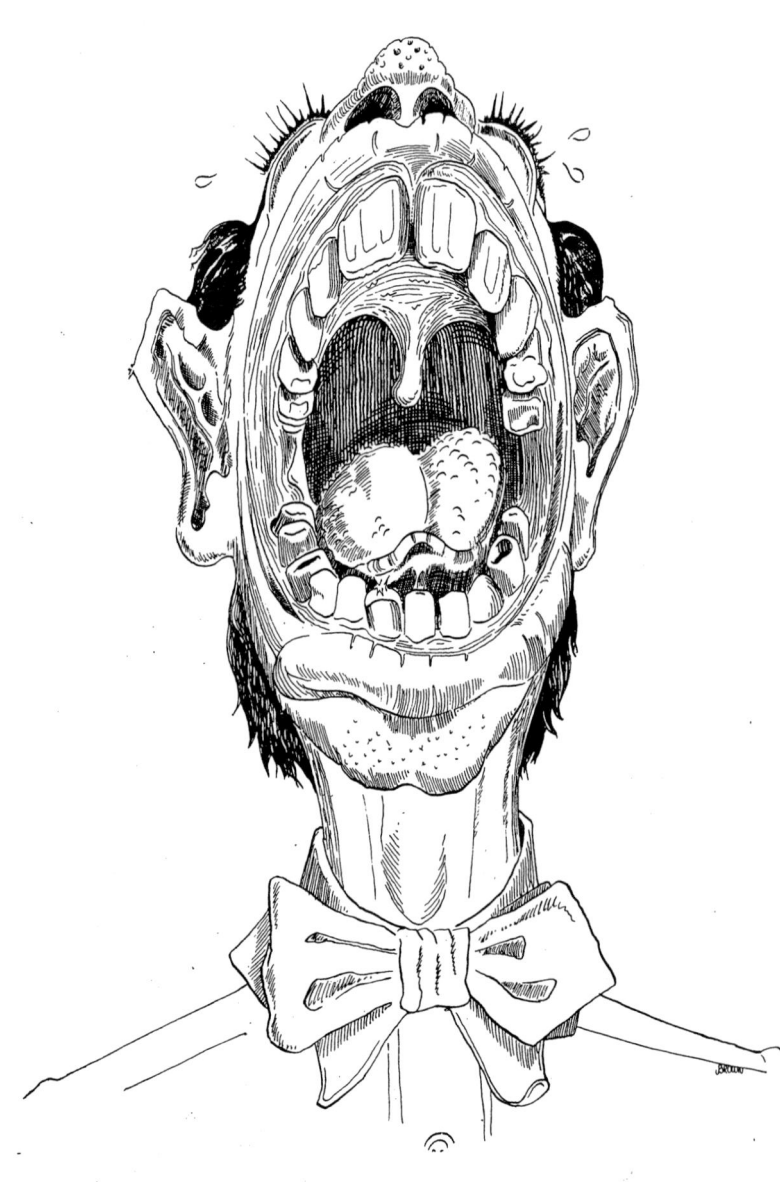

Loud singing is loud speech, or a controlled shout

The shout is a most helpful device to use. Pitch it high, and ask choir members to see how well they can project it. You'll be gratified to see them use their new technique (diaphragm) in an effort to get more power (volume). Next, have them sustain the shout on a fairly high pitch (E-F-G). When they can do this well, it is only a short step to harnessing their newfound energy to a chord or phrase. The toughest problem they face will probably be overcoming their natural inhibitions. It's not easy to shout at the top of your lungs when there's no game on. But once you get them in the spirit of it, you're on the way.

Can they shout incorrectly? They certainly can, and you must watch and listen carefully in order to detect and correct the screamer. You might try "hah" or "hey" for the shout. If the jaw is down and the throat open, they will do no harm to their voices.

4. What to Teach About Vowels and Consonants

Speak the speech, I pray you,
as I pronounced it to you,
trippingly on the tongue.
        WILLIAM SHAKESPEARE, 1564–1616

What to Teach About Vowels and Consonants

THE APPROACH TO VOWELS involves two basic decisions by the conductor:
1. Which vowel sounds, or colors, are the most beautiful and/or most nearly correct.
2. How he is going to communicate his choice to his singers.

Notice the phrase "most beautiful and/or most nearly correct." There is a wide divergence of opinion among us as to just what the most pleasing vowel color is. Some conductors prefer a bright, forward placement with a good deal of "ring" or "ping" in the sound. Others like a deep-set placement further back in the mouth and throat for maximum mellowness. Many others will vary the vowel placement, depending on the text and mood of the music.

The overriding consideration would seem to be the word "correct." No vowel color should be acceptable that does violence to the singing apparatus. The acid test of any vocal technique is how well the voice endures with its use. Apparently a good singing technique can be maintained through a fairly wide adjustment of vowel color, so the conductor must decide what, for him, is the most satisfying sound.

In addition to beauty of tone (and that's what vowel color is all about), there is the matter of blend. We talk about "aligning" or "unifying" the vowel. This simply refers to the process of getting all the singers to enunciate the vowels in the same way (color). The choir with a wide variety of vowel concepts is a poorly blended, or more accurately, an unblended choir. But let's go back to step 1—deciding on the colors or placement.

Some of us have never given much thought to what we like or don't like in vowel color, especially if our vocal background is limited. We teach the notes and rhythm and accept the resulting sound as the natural product of our particular combination of voices. Such an acceptance means that we have an almost negligible influence on the kind of choral sound our group produces simply because *we* don't have a sound goal in our minds. Perhaps the best way to remedy this is to begin listening carefully and analytically to recordings and live performances of a wide variety of good choirs. What is distinctive about them? What is their concept of vowel color? Is their sound bright or dark, "edgy" or "woofy," satisfying or disconcerting? Why do they sound as they do? You will soon discover that the basic sound of any group is largely due to the vowel colors they are using. It is but a short step from intelligent listening to some basic decisions. In short, what sounds do you find the most beautiful and satisfying?

It is not the purpose of this book to argue the case for a particular vocal approach, although of course I have convictions on the subject. The point is to explain the need for our forming some conclusions with this simple suggestion of how to do it.

As difficult as developing a philosophy of tone may be, it is even harder to communicate the concepts to lay singers. To begin with, the language is vague. We use terms like "dark, bright, focus, woofy, forward, nasal, throaty, deep-set"—all of which may be explicit to us, but which may mean many different things to others. We must begin by clarifying the vocabulary we are going to use. An even greater obstacle is the fact that we do not hear ourselves as others hear us. Our singers may be trying very hard to produce the sound requested, and probably think they are doing so, only to be told they are not matching the desired color. That is why the finest singers you know still study voice. They recognize the need for an objective set of ears to tell them whether they are doing what they think they are doing.

To dramatize this point for yourself and your choir, ask everyone on one row to sing a given pitch on a given vowel, for instance, middle C on an "ah." Have them sing one at a time quickly down the row. The result will be almost as many versions of the "ah" as there are people on the row—and they all will be convinced they sang it just as you did! Obviously, no blend is possible until everyone sings every vowel in essentially the same way. Naturally, the more beautiful the vowel sounds selected, the more beautiful the choral sound produced.

Once having decided on the basic vowel sounds and having assured ourselves that they are consistent with good vocal production, we are faced with the task of teaching them to our singers. The problems vary somewhat with the speech habits of the different sections of the country. The deep South has one set of problems, while the Southwest has another, and the East has still another. It is safe to say, however, that the malady common to most is the closed mouth and throat. While voice teachers disagree on many points of technique, nearly all agree on the basic position of the singing mechanism—lowered, relaxed jaw, and high, arched soft palate. This formation, called the "singer's throat," allows for relaxation and spaciousness in the two primary resonating areas, the mouth and the throat. Most of us fail to get these areas open enough, resulting in a thin, "white" sound. The opposite condition, a dark, swallowed tone, occurs occasionally; but it is less often encountered. Consequently, we shall concentrate on the more common habits and confine the discussion to the open vowels since they are the most commonly sinned against.

THE JAW—It seems natural to start our work with the jaw. It is easily accessible, and the results are immediate and dramatic. A tried and true method that has been around for years will serve us well here. Have the singers place the first and second fingers on edge between the front teeth. This spacing will serve as a good approximation for the "ah" vowel, with minor adjustments for one's individual physiognomy. There are two immediate problems: (1) we cannot sing Sunday's anthem with our fingers in our mouths, and (2) without them, the jaw tends to close to its usual, barely open position. It takes constant reminding and a lot of "fingers-in-mouth" exercises before our singers finally realize that they, in fact, do not open their mouths adequately when they sing. Although it will feel strange and decidedly ungraceful to them, it is an essential step toward freeing the sound.

THE THROAT—Since most of us cannot get our hands in our throats, the approach here needs to be less mechanical and more mental. The singer must concentrate on keeping the tongue down in back (say "ah"). He might *think* about the beginning of a yawn, or he might *imagine* he has a light bulb in his mouth with the small end pointing out. Our goal is the same whatever the imagery employed—an open, spacious throat that provides maximum resonating space for the sound.

Once the mouth and throat are established for "ah," we have a point of reference for "oh." By maintaining that spaciousness and rounding the lips, we can produce a rich, resonant vowel. Round the lips a bit more and we have the "oo." At first, the singers will have difficulty maintaining the roominess in the mouth and throat. Go back to the "ah" and start over. It will take time and will require constant reminding, but this one accomplishment can transform the sound of a choir. Coupled with breath support, the deep-set, open vowel is fundamental to beautiful tone.

A benefit from the open throat and mouth, beyond the increased resonance, is improved breath support. Many singers use their chewing and swallowing muscles to start and stop the flow of air. With these out of the way, the diaphragm more easily assumes its rightful role, a worthwhile goal of any vocal technique.

The other vowels are worthy of a book all their own. If we can achieve a really open freedom on "ah," "oh," and "oo," however, we will have taken a giant step toward a more beautiful choral sound as well as a viable vocal technique.

Since we are dealing with both Adult and Youth choirs here, a question might logically be raised regarding different approaches for different age groups. It seems to me that any technique that produces singing that is beautiful, open, and free is a worthy technique for any age. Pure vowels are pure vowels, whatever the age of the mechanism producing them, and serve equally as well for the child as the adult or teen. Some argue that to strive for deep-set vowels in younger voices is to attempt to make them sound like adults. Nonsense! The objective is to unleash all the beauty and resonance inherent in the voice at any given stage of its development. There are conductors who attempt to make their young singers sound older by employing a swallowed, "woofy" production, often with rather dramatic results. To my ear, however, the sound is forced and artificial, and not especially beautiful. In my judgment this method falls short of the criteria given here; therefore, I do not consider it a viable option.

The fact that the singer does not hear himself accurately or that he may have a misconception of the actual vowel sound bears repeating with this suggestion. Sometimes you may achieve a desired vowel color by demonstrating the sound a shade darker (or lighter) than you really want. In his effort to duplicate this exaggerated color, the amateur singer will often come much closer to making the sound you really want. It is devious, but often effective.

Consonants

Years ago I heard a wise old conductor say, "If vowels tell what you mean, then consonants tell how much you mean it." This comment has haunted and helped me ever since. I think he was trying to say that while the vowels are responsible for beauty of word, tone, and line, the consonants provide degree of meaning, particularly for verbs.

You can illustrate this very simply to your choir members. Have them say the word "hate" in a normal tone of voice with average consonant power. Then without changing the volume, have them say it again with a heavily aspirated *h* and a sharply exploded *t*. They have suddenly transformed a routine dislike into a red rage, and without even raising their voices. Then try the same experiment with the word "love," varying the stress on the *l* and *v*. The results are the same, but it is a lot more fun.

That lesson will not be lost on the choir. Even the uninitiated will perceive that drama, excitement, and vitality, not to mention precision and intelligibility, are communicated largely through the consonants. What a welcome alternative for those who have always just screamed a little louder when emphasis was needed. Nor should we permit our singers to become lazy as the dynamic level drops. If anything, a *decrescendo* should have a corresponding *increase* in consonant energy. This will help keep the text intelligible as the sound gets soft; more importantly, it will combat the tendency to allow the tone to become limp, flat, and nonvital.

In our zeal for clean, precise singing, is it possible to overdo the consonants? It certainly is. I recall judging a splendid high-school choir some years ago that did nearly everything right. They had magnificent tone (vowels), balance, and blend. Their shortcoming? Why, the consonants were so violently articulated you could hardly hear the singing for the noise they made! They were performing a highly contrapuntal number and literally inundated their audience with pops, hisses, and saliva. Was the diction precise and understandable? Certainly. But the excessive consonant racket destroyed a potentially brilliant performance.

How, then, can we discuss consonants with our choir members without appearing to be ambiguous and contradictory? Suggest this simple principle: Except for reasons of special effect, the consonant should be just strong enough to make the word intelligible. Anything less produces mushy diction; anything more results in extraneous, nonmusical noise.

In addition to degree of energy, there are other common errors when dealing with consonants. The final consonant is frequently anticipated, always with unhappy results. An anticipated "stop" consonant will naturally shorten the note value assigned to the word involved and will invariably cause the singer to hurry into the next word. Others will be anticipated and then sounded for the duration, often with unpleasant or noisy vocal results. In that event, choir members will need to be reminded to do their singing on the vowels, with the final consonant actually terminating the note value.

Also common is the imploding (stopping or "turning in") of explosive consonants, as we frequently do in speaking. That is done in ignorance or with the mistaken idea that the musical line will be more *legato* without the little percussive interruptions. Actually, the opposite is the case. The implosion will cause a complete stop of the sound, while a normal execution will fill the gaps with action. *Legato* singing can better be served by carefully eliding the consonants in appropriate situations. This means dividing a word in such a way as to place the final consonant of one word at the beginning of the next word (res-tin-peace). This practice tends to connect words that otherwise would be detached.

The companion voiced and unvoiced consonants can provide some interesting pronunciations when used incorrectly. These are pairs of consonants that are formed the same way but differ in the use or nonuse of the vocal mechanism. That is, one of the twins will require phonation in order to differentiate it from its partner. Here is a list of consonants which indicates their voiced or unvoiced status.

Unvoiced	*Voiced*
f	v
t	d
s	z
wh	w
p	b
th (as in *th*imble)	th (as in *th*ere)
k	g (as in got)
sh	s (as in pleasure)
ch	j
	g (as in Geoffrey)
h	(no partner)

Even after your brilliantly lucid explanations, some choir members will continue to sing, "I' *braying* for you," "*Gum*, Thou Almighty King," "When morning *kilts* the sky," "Why do you *wade*, dear brother?" "We *braise* Thee, O God!" and on and on. Perhaps the simplest way to illustrate the difference is by having them try to whisper the consonant. If they can do it successfully, then obviously the vocal cords are not needed (we do not use the cords in a whisper), and the consonant is an unvoiced one. If they attempt to whisper a voiced consonant, however, they quickly discover it comes out like its voiceless partner. Only with the addition of the voice will these consonants sound correctly.

It doesn't take a Ph. D. in English to realize that the proper treatment of these partners is important indeed if we are to be understood at all.

Blend

We have discussed the role of the vowel as a twofold one, relating both to the quality of the sound and the blend of the ensemble. While vowel unification is probably the best first step toward choral blend, it is not the last; and the alert conductor must always be working toward that "homogenized" sound. After unification, his next consideration may well be the treatment of *vibrato* in the group.

Here is another subject that can incite heated debates among voice teachers and choralists. Some believe that there is no room for a *vibrato* in a choral group, while others hold that any tampering with it is dangerous or heretical, or both. The best solution, again, lies somewhere in the middle.

It is impossible to tune an unusual *vibrato* (too wide, fast, or slow) simply because you are never sure which of the resulting pitches to tune to. The unusual *vibrato* is so distinctive that, like the unusual vowel sound, it is difficult to submerge into the ensemble. Obviously, then, this kind of voice will require some "straightening" if it is to be blended with those around it.

On the other hand, to remove all *vibrato* from the tone is to lessen its warmth, color, and variety. To be sure, some kinds of music are more stylistically satisfying if done with a minimum of *vibrato*—Renaissance, some contemporary, pop, and would you believe, barbershop, to name a few. However, I would reserve this vocal approach for a specific stylistic effect rather than use it as a general, all-inclusive philosophy. I know of no instances of voice damage from straight tone singing, but it does require more air and more rigid control.

It is at this point that some voice teachers protest the loudest at having their students sing in a choral group. They feel, perhaps with justification, that some choralists ask for vocal adjustments that are contrary to good vocal technique. This is the precise reason why we must be certain that the sound we want (vowels, *vibrato*, etc.) is consistent with good singing habits.

Any voice can be made to blend with any other. It's just a matter of whittling away at their respective uniqueness until they sound alike. If we do very much of this, however, we produce a stark, sterile sound with the likelihood of poor vocal technique, all in the name of blend. It would seem to be a worthwhile goal to attempt to achieve an acceptable blend with a minimum of personal adjustment by the individual singers.

At this point the seating arrangement within a section can be of unusual significance. Most directors are fairly specific about the seating of the respective sections, but often permit the placement of individual singers just to happen. Choir members choose their seats because of their height, to be with their friends, to avoid a draft, to "lean" on a strong singer, and for a variety of other nonmusical reasons. Yet a careful appraisal of individual voices can often simplify and hasten the blending process.

The idea is to put like voices together insofar as it is possible. You can determine which voices are similar by having them sing a phrase or two of a hymn, individually. After they have recovered from the shock, choose from the section a voice that is accurate, fairly lyric in nature, and with no unusual vocal characteristics. Make that person "anchor man" for the section. He will not necessarily have the best voice, and certainly not the biggest, but it will be a voice with no eccentricities, one to which other singers can easily adjust. His seat will be on the end of the section toward the center of the choir. After the "anchor man" is established, have the individuals in the section take turns singing a phrase or two with him, making no particular effort to adjust or blend while doing so. The person making the best combination with the No. 1 man becomes the No. 2 man. Then the entire process is repeated while you search for the voice that goes best with No. 2 (No. 1 is no longer involved), and so on until the whole section is seated from the inside of the choir out. If more than one row is required, the process is still the same, with the lighter, more lyric voices in the center, and the bigger, more powerful voices toward the ends. This technique takes a little time, but the results are amazing and well worth the effort. You can generally achieve an excellent blend with a minimum of individual vocal compromise and accommodation. This is because everyone is singing beside voices with which he is comfortable, and he no longer has to work so hard at blending.

There are two obvious drawbacks to all this voice matching. One is the matter of height, which can create some perfectly ludicrous situations, especially if your risers are short. The other is absenteeism, which can absolutely demolish your beautiful playhouse. Nevertheless, voice matching is a quick, easy, and natural way to blended singing. It is well worth any time and effort invested in it.

5. Conducting

I don't recall your name, but your manners are familiar.
　　　　　Oliver Herford, 1863–1935

5. Conducting

WITH ALL THE THINGS we must cram into our precious rehearsal time, should we really try to teach conducting, too? The answer is yes and no. As far as teaching members to conduct, the answer is no. As commendable as that objective might be, there is just no time in *choir rehearsal* to do it. (A separate study, perhaps?) But if we are talking about teaching the *language* of conducting to our singers, then the answer is a resounding "Yes!"

Few of us ever take the time to discuss the mysteries of those graceful arcs and swirls with the very people who are supposed to respond instantly and precisely to them. Here is one more area where a little time spent "teaching" can pay huge dividends in rehearsal time saved and performances improved. Most of us seem to expect the choir members just to *know* what it all means. Because we know what we mean by our gestures, we seem to assume that they know as well. This is a naïve assumption indeed. Conducting is a highly skilled and complex art. It is the language of the conductor as surely as the notation is the

... the mysteries of those graceful arcs and swirls

language of the composer. It would behoove us, then, to make certain that the language is clearly "spoken" by the conductor and readily understood by the follower. Note once more that the burden *begins* with the leader, and all of us need to constantly scrutinize our conducting habits to make certain that we are not the source of the problem.

If our object is not to make conductors out of our singers, just what areas should we discuss with them? Which techniques, if explained, would shed the most light on the language? How far do we pursue the techniques involved? May I suggest some areas.

If a choir is to attack (and release) with precision, the members must see and understand a properly executed preparation beat. It should tell them three things:
1. The tempo of the music to follow
2. The approximate dynamic level to be sung
3. Something of the style of the music

The importance of the first is easily demonstrated by giving them several "out of tempo" preparatory beats. In other words, give a very languid preparation, then take off on a much faster tempo when you get to the downbeat. Then reverse the problem by conducting a quick preparation followed by a very deliberate tempo. The resulting raggedness dramatizes the importance of the preparatory beat as the indicator of the forthcoming tempo. Of course, you will then demonstrate the proper preparatory beat (that you always use) which is *in* the tempo that is desired.

The volume of the music is indicated by the size of the preparatory beat. If the attack is *forte* or above, the gesture would be relatively big and forceful. If the music is to be quiet, the preparatory beat would be small. Again, you may want to demonstrate the capacity of this simple gesture to communicate by doing it incorrectly a few times.

Something of the style of the music can also be telegraphed

as well. The quick, incisive move or the graceful flowing wrist can remind us of the *staccato* or *legato* nature of the music to come. Choir members quickly learn how much can be inferred from these gestures. Equally as quickly, they will tell us when sloppy execution has misled them. As our teaching takes root, our conducting must stay honest.

Another area important to a choir is the beat point (*ictus*). It is that place in the pattern that marks the precise beginning of each beat. Occasionally you will hear musicians complain that they can't see the beat. They probably are not referring to the pattern itself (a different problem). They really mean that the beat points are so indistinguishable that they can't discern where one beat stops and a new one starts. The rhythmic integrity of a performance will depend on a clearly defined *ictus*. Without it, both note values and tempo become erratic.

Closely related to the *ictus* is the reflex, or rebound. It is just that, a slight springing away from the *ictus* that actually helps define the *ictus*. To demonstrate its functions and importance, beat a few patterns with no rebound whatever. Choir members may never have noticed this little motion before, but they will see immediately that without it the beats are wooden and unpredictable. The *ictus* and rebound are kissing cousins, and their clear definition is essential to legible conducting.

A violinist friend told me of playing for a conductor whose downbeat was notably lacking in *ictus* or rebound. When asked how the orchestra managed to come in, he replied, "It wasn't easy, but we finally agreed among ourselves that when the stick reached the third button on his vest, we'd play!" That is not a recommended technique.

The choir needs to understand that beats start with the *ictus* and last *until the next ictus*. An understanding of this point may help combat the tendency to cheat note values, particularly those followed by rests.

The third gesture of special importance is the release. When it is misunderstood for any reason, the results can be catastrophic. If it *is* misunderstood, it may be due to faulty execution on your part; so before you start explaining it, check yourself on these points.

1. The release needs to be adequately prepared just as an attack does. We've all seen conductors who cut off chords or phrases so suddenly that the singers straggled off in poise-shattering disarray. One or two experiences like that and choir members begin to lose confidence in the release (or the conductor). Rather than be left hanging again, they start thinking about stopping the moment they get to a phrase end, regardless of the note value. This means that instead of a solid, confident phrase end (assuming that's what is written), the volume begins to fall off immediately, and all because of the quick-draw artist on the podium. It is not considered a virtue to keep the singers guessing. Telegraph your intention to terminate the sound. Prepare the release so that they may sustain and/or cut off with assurance.

2. Another thing to bear in mind is the size or strength of the release. The rule here is simply to make it in the context of the music. If the music is loud and vigorous, then a sturdy release is in order. If the music is quiet and gentle, a less vigorous gesture is appropriate. This is a simple rule, but its violation can have unfortunate consequences. A quiet phrase that is cut off too vigorously can result in a harsh or explosive release. The small and understrength gesture applied to a big passage just may not get the job done at all. Make the release in character and in tempo, and everyone is happy.

2. The release must possess the same *ictus* and rebound that characterize a good beat, otherwise the singer cannot discern the precise moment when the sound should stop. In other words, the release, like the beat, should possess exactness and predictability. In all of conducting, this is the most unfavorable place to be making "lazy circles in the sky."

...the quick draw artist on the podium

Perhaps the greatest friend of amateur singers is the cue. As uncertain readers, they respond eagerly and gratefully to a look and gesture in their direction. In the course of teaching about the sign language, we need to explain the cue, when it will and will not come, and how we will likely execute it. Let's review what we are going to tell them.

Begin by explaining what a cue is not. It is not an exercise in dexterity for two hands. It is not an opportunity to impress the congregation with how complicated the music or the conducting is. It is not to give us something to do besides beating the pattern. It has one role, and that is to provide security and assurance to an entrance.

"When can we expect to see it?" they ask. When the choir or their section enters for the first time; or after a lengthy rest; or if the rhythm is difficult; or if the entrance is loud (thereby requiring special courage); and in a few other assorted places.

"Goody!" they exclaim. "But tell us, O Wise One, what does this marvelous gesture look like?"

Now we sagely explain that the cue is given with the right hand within the beat pattern, with the left hand, or if both are otherwise occupied, with the eyes and a nod of the head. (You'd better practice this one privately before trying it, lest you throw something out of joint.)

Let me suggest some things about the cue that will help it be of maximum effectiveness. First, like the attack and release, it needs preparation. The cue that comes shooting out at a choir member at the precise moment he should be singing is of little assurance. If the entrance is made at all, it may well be late and rather explosive. Be certain that adequate warning (preparation) is given. This ingredient called assurance is provided mainly by the eyes. (We're still talking about amateurs.) It is the eye contact that tells not only that an entrance is to be made, but also by whom. I can't overstress this point. A small gesture accompanied by a look will provide twice the security

... lest you throw something out of joint

of a large gesture delivered while the head is down in the music. By our example we can teach one of the most difficult lessons of all, that of watching the director. Why look at a director who never looks back? If we want their eyes, we must give them ours, certainly on the cues if at no other time. Make a date with them for those special entrances. Tell them you will be looking at them and that you expect them to be looking back. It's a great way to develop a watching choir, providing, of course, that they have something to see other than the top of your head.

One last point. Be consistent. If you cue it in rehearsal, make certain you cue it in performance. Once they learn to look for a cue, they tend to become dependent on it. To forget it is to risk a blown entrance, regardless of how well they know the music. The cue is one of the most helpful gestures you can provide the volunteer singer. Learn it well and dispense it generously.

Many of us who start out as fairly competent conductors find that the needs of volunteer singers tend to erode that carefully nurtured technique we learned in school. We find ourselves gradually beating bigger and harder and singing louder and louder. If these gestures are in fact a language, then many of us are always shouting at our singers. If we want to teach our choirs to sing musically, we must conduct musically. Three watchdogs can serve us well. We'll name them efficiency, economy, and clarity.

Flamboyant conducting may be well received in some concert halls, but it is particularly distracting in church. There, of all places, the dialogue between conductor and choir should be a private, even intimate one. It behooves us, then, to make sure our gestures mean what they say, and to the proper degree.

A little cliché that has been around for a long time says something to the effect that our conducting should "look like the music." That has much merit. It is telling us to use no more gesture than the music at any given point would suggest.

Unfortunately, we allow our choir to push us into inefficient conducting. We make a moderate gesture for an entrance of modest strength, and no one comes in. The next time, we hit them with a mighty sweep of the arm, and *eureka*, we get our *mezzo-piano* entrance. So far so good, at least until that *forte* entrance comes along. Naturally we must distinguish it from the *mezzo-piano* entrance, so we make mighty sweeps with both arms. Success again, but, ah, the *fortissimo* climax approaches. We must spur them to greater effort, so with arms flailing, face flushing, veins throbbing, eyes bugging, knees bobbing, voice screaming, and sweat running down, we extract the *fortissimo* from our reluctant troops. Where did we go wrong? Back there at the *mezzo-piano*.

Dynamic levels are relative to each other, and efficient conducting reflects that relativity. Once we permit the size and strength of our gestures to become mismatched or out of phase with the musical requirements, then we have become inefficient conductors. We are using cannon to shoot mice, as it were. The antidote? Train the choir members to respond to the appropriate gestures. Insist on it, and soon you will have a group that is sensitive and responsive to your every move. This is part of the curriculum. To fail to teach it is to risk a coronary at every *fortissimo*. Efficient conducting means maximum response to a minimum of effort.

Our second watchdog, economy, is brother to efficiency, and they are often difficult to separate. In order to keep this dialogue as private as possible, we must strive for an economy of motion. Keeping the pattern centered in front of the body between the eyes and the waist, we should again make certain that the amount of motion is consistent with the music involved. Avoid big patterns if small ones are sufficient. Don't use both hands if one is ample. Don't bob and weave if the only one who feels better for it is you.

The place for most of us to begin an economy drive would

Three watchdogs ... efficiency, economy, clarity

likely be with the left hand. This faithful servant is much used and abused, and all interests would be served if it were reserved for its rightful role. The most common error is habitual beat doubling. The left hand simply duplicates the right with no particular purpose served. The problem here is that when those big, *maestoso* passages come, the presence of the left hand has no special significance. The choir member has seen it too much already. Better that we save the doubling for those passages.

The matter of cueing, certainly a legitimate province of the left hand, can also be overdone. Most routine cues can be handled smoothly and economically with the right hand, *within the beat pattern*. When the left hand *is* employed, its use is attention grabbing indeed, and vital entrances can be strongly reinforced with it. The same is true for releases. If the left hand is held in reserve for those special purposes it serves best, its use will carry twice the impact, and the rest of the conducting will be far less cluttered and far more economical.

Another common sight on the festival circuit is the singing conductor. Undoubtedly a crusade against this practice would be more futile than tilting with windmills, but discussions on efficiency and economy would be incomplete without a few words on the subject.

Here again we can attribute a bad habit to an insecure choir. (Convenient, isn't it?) The basses don't read, the tenors didn't show, the sopranos are lost, etc., so we leap into the gap. Four things ought to be realized at this point.

1. Your contribution is of limited value to a person several feet away who is also singing. Maybe he hears you, maybe not.

2. The biggest difference you have made in the overall sound is the way it appears to *you*. You have supplied a missing line, or corrected or strengthened a part for your ear, and things sound a lot better *to you*. Besides, that glorious voice of yours would dramatically improve any choir.

3. When you are singing loudly you can't hear thunder,

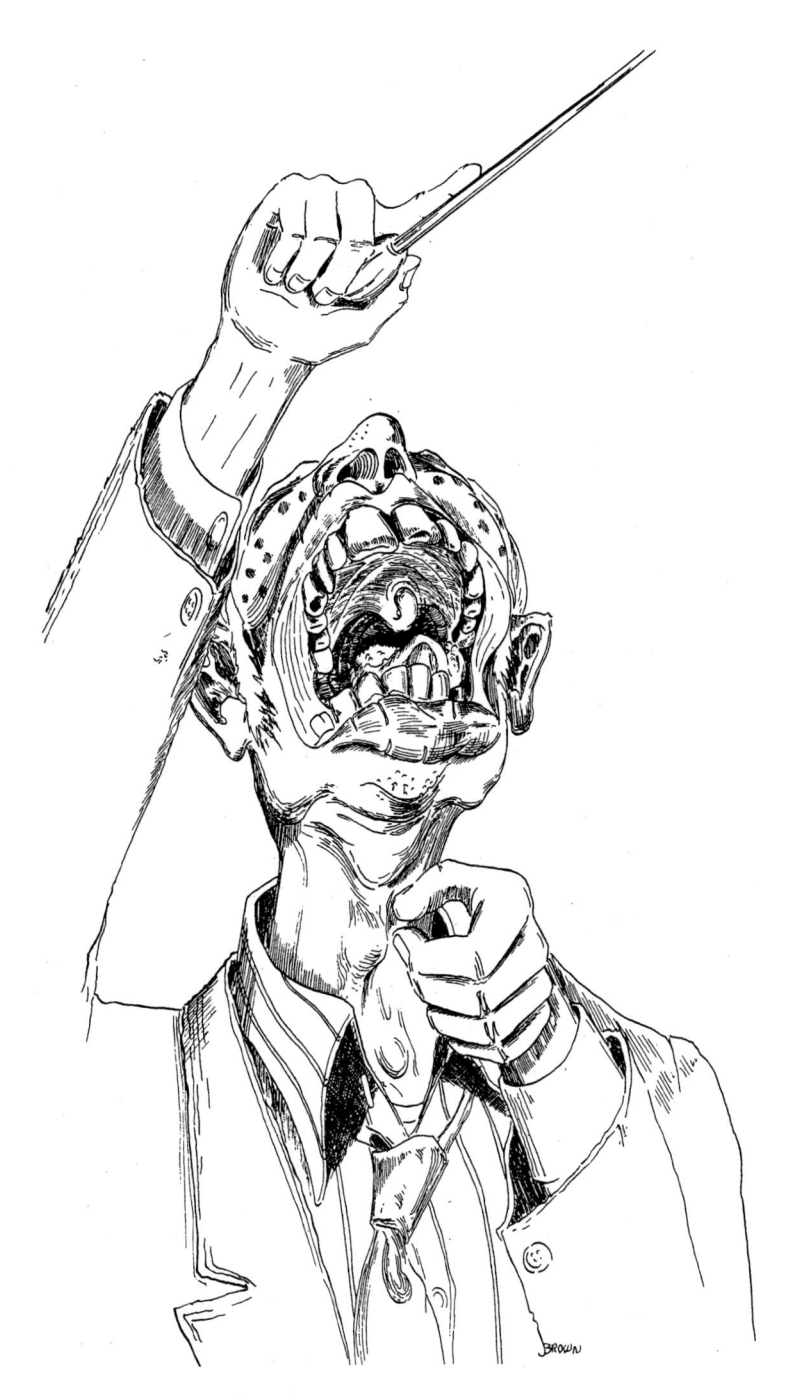

The singing conductor

much less small imperfections in the choir. Consequently you are abdicating your primary responsibility as "the big ear," a risky practice with often shocking ramifications.

4. Worst of all, you have stopped leading with your hands and begun pulling with your voice, making your hands a redundant accessory after the fact. Although many of us do it, it is really pretty tough to make a good case for singing with the choir.

Some of us have licked the habit of singing along, but we still mouth the words. This, too, is a useless and not very becoming habit. If they have the words in front of them, they don't need help from you. If the sections have different words, you have problems; besides, you just might mouth the wrong words, which doesn't help a bit. There is really no point in cluttering the "language" with what can be a rather distracting habit. It's probably another case of making us feel more effectual rather than actually helping the choir, but it is redundant and uneconomical.

The third watchdog is clarity, and he is the most important of all. In the final analysis, our conducting is effective in direct proportion to its legibility. It must be clean, clear, understandable, and unambiguous. Conducting that requires lengthy explanations is self-defeating, and one of the nicest compliments we can receive is that we are easy to follow. And now abideth efficiency, economy, and clarity; these three. But the greatest of these is clarity!

The cause of economy is served by negating the beat when the musical action is at a relatively low level. In other words, the size of the pattern should not only reflect the dynamic level of the music; it can also change size according to the amount of resources employed at a given moment. Suppose the full choir should give way to a solo line for sopranos. A smaller pattern could well be in order. Or what do we do for organ interludes? One moment we are conducting thirty singers, and the next, only one. It would be a bit wasteful to conduct in mighty strokes for a single hundred-and-twenty-pound organist, regardless of how lovely she is playing. Also, the choir singing sustained notes over a moving accompaniment does not require a normal-sized pattern. In fact, we might very well fool them into singing at the wrong time if our pattern shows no distinction between active and static situations.

The negated pattern is not a lifeless one. It contains all the attributes of a normal beating, including impulse of will. It is simply scaled down in size in order to reflect a smaller degree of musical action, and contributes not only to economy of motion, but to clarity and efficiency as well.

The matter of being a convincing leader is never more crucial than when we are actually conducting. At this stage we are totally dependent on our gestures to communicate for us. We can hardly stop for a lecture during the performance. It's important, then, that we speak this language not only clearly and precisely but forcefully as well. It is not uncommon to see conductors whose technique is well thought out and whose gestures are technically correct. Everything is there and it is readable, but the choir responds sluggishly or not at all. Why? Very likely it's because the conducting lacks forcefulness or authority. The singers see it, but they don't really believe it. It is unconvincing. It lacks positiveness.

Several words are frequently used to describe that particular ingredient in conductors. We call it forcefulness or authority or dynamism, or perhaps just poise. The most expressive term I have encountered is one coined by Maestro Nicholai Malko. He called it "impulse of will." Whatever we label it, we all know what it is and are aware of how absolutely essential it is to one's conducting if the conducting is to be followed with any confidence. With it, the technique is assured and commanding. Without it, the conducting appears tentative and apologetic.

The amount of impulse of will required varies with the desired response from the choir. A flowing *legato* may require very little, while a syncopated passage may require much more. A difficult or exposed entrance is made confidently only with considerable impulse of will from the conductor. Nor would one wave lethargically at a very big and/or important release. If we are expecting something important to happen as a result of our gesture, we must make certain it contains enough authority to get the job done.

Occasionally we see conductors with impulse of will to spare, but nothing else. In other words, there is great vitality and forcefulness but no technique or *finesse*. That kind of conducting frequently has great potential, but it will never be realized unless this dynamism is harnessed and controlled by a disciplined technique.

These are the areas I consider most important for discussion with, and demonstration to, the choir. They do not release us from the responsibility of conducting good patterns, or for doing all those other things related to good conducting that have not been discussed here. I mention these areas because I feel they can be quickly taught, easily grasped by the layman, and immediately translated into more precise, confident performances by the choir members because you have helped them understand the sign language. One word of caution. The more knowledgeable your singers become, the more observant they will be. This means that they can be critical of sloppy conducting or appreciative of good technique. Make sure your conducting is as good as your teaching.

On Conducting Instrumentalists

The use of band and orchestra instruments is becoming increasingly common and desirable in our churches. This practice presents some special conducting problems that we should consider. This is not to suggest that conducting instrumentalists is a whole new ball game, for it isn't. A clean, precise gesture-language developed for the singer is perfectly adequate for the instrumentalist. In fact, you will probably find the instrumentalist more attentive and responsive to you than your singers. He simply has a different set of problems, and the choral conductor needs to acquaint himself with those problems in order to deal with them intelligently during a rehearsal or performance.

The best way to introduce yourself to the problems involved is to take a good look at a part for one of the instruments. You will see that the page is filled by single staves devoted to that one part. Except for occasional brief cues, the player has no clue as to what the other instrumentalists are doing. There are no words to help him follow the progress of the singer. Some measures contain nothing more than a rest with a number indicating how many measures of rest are to be observed. Obviously, this relatively sparse amount of information given is a far cry from the choral score clutched in the sweaty palms of the singer. He not only has his own part, but all the other parts as well, plus the keyboard accompaniment. If he should get lost, and/or the conductor is inept, he has a great deal of information to help him reorient himself. Not so the instrumentalist with his single, wordless line.

The awareness of that single-line score should suggest three things to the conductor.

1. The instrumentalist must rely almost totally on the counting of passing measures in order to keep his place in the music. This means the pattern in general and the downbeat in particular must always be legible to him. Choral conductors are often in error at this point. We can become so enamored of the beautiful phrases we are sculpting in the air that the pattern is virtually nonexistent. That can make it pretty difficult for the player who is not sure where he is in the score.

2. It is important to indicate the passage of *all* beats and *all*

... they can be very critical of sloppy conducting

measures. Again, we choralists tend to get careless. We arrive at a whole note, or perhaps two or three of them tied together, so we stop the beat for a season and then resume when the spirit moves us. There is no problem for the singers. They know exactly what you are doing. But imagine how that looks to a trumpet player in the middle of a 32-bar rest. When the beat resumes, he has no way of knowing which measure you are conducting. How much clearer the conducting is when the beat is scrupulously continued, especially if a smaller, negated pattern is used for the sake of economy.

The same thing is true of rests and incomplete measures. Remember that the player is counting madly in order to keep his place, especially if he is "resting." The conductor who fails to indicate the passage of rested beats, whether for whole or partial measures, can generate a gigantic and potentially disastrous guessing game among the philharmonic. If it's on the page, conduct it.

3. We must understand that the role of the cue takes on special significance for the instrumentalist. He may read and count more accurately than the average singer, but he is also likely to have much longer rests between passages. The cymbal player who has dropped his music, waved a fly off his nose, and located his girl friend in the audience while counting out a 93-bar rest is appreciative indeed when the maestro nods in his direction at the appointed time. He plays with verve and assurance because he and the conductor seem to agree on precisely where that dramatic crash is to occur. This is a good thing, for it is difficult to play the cymbals hesitantly. The point, of course, is that the longer the rest and the louder the entrance, the more desirable the cue. Of course those instrumentalists are good musicians, but they will play with greater poise and assurance if they are cued as conscientiously as the singers are.

You will also need to be precise with your verbal directions. A page number or a line of the text may be fine to orient the choir member, but will not mean a thing to the trombonist. The instrumentalist will require the mention of special musical landmarks to help him determine where you are. These include measure numbers, key or meter changes, double bars, fermatas, etc.

Obviously, the director who intends to involve himself frequently and seriously with instruments should have more than a nodding acquaintance with them. He should learn about their transpositions, capabilities, and difficulties if he is to be an effective conductor of instrumentalists. This is not so say that the neophite should not undertake the conducting of occasional instrumental accompaniment. On the contrary, if he has competent players and is thoroughly prepared, he will probably function adequately.

A word about those "competent players." The less knowledgeable we are, the more intimidated we seem to be by the experienced player. That is natural, but self-defeating. The veteran player can look out for himself and his own problems, whereas the beginners may turn to you for help you are simply unequipped to give. If you are a beginner with instrumentalists, seek every possible opportunity to work with experienced players. They will perform better and be of immense help to you, especially if you listen to their timely suggestions and don't pretend to know more about the situation than you actually do.

6. Interpretation

I wish there were windows to my soul,
so that you could see some of
my feelings.
     Artemus Ward, 1834–1867

6. Interpretation

OF ALL THE TASKS the conductor faces, none is more capable of creating insecurity than that of interpretation. This is especially true in the case of the novice. Long after we have mastered the mechanics of the printed page, we agonize over the phrases and musical nuances, wondering whether we are "doing it right." Perhaps that is why we tend to rehash, over and over, the music we learned in someone else's choir. We *know* how to do it because someone else showed us. How can we teach interpretation to a choir if *we* are insecure and tentative?

Obviously we cannot. In order to arrive at a method of presentation to the choir, we must organize an approach to the music for ourselves. (You may have noticed by now that throughout the book the teaching process is based on our own grasp and organization of the subject matter. If we can but chart our own course through the problems and then articulate that course lucidly, we have a good chance of making ourselves understood by choir members.)

Our approach to interpreting choral music is twofold:

through the text and through the music itself, in that order. How else can we start except by determining what the text is all about? Separate it from the music. Read it as poetry. If there are unfamiliar words, look them up. Know what the writer is saying.

If the text has been skilfully set, the music will enhance and underscore the words . . . else why set it at all? For this is one of music's great attributes—the ability to heighten and amplify the word, to focus attention, and to turn the text so that its different facets may reflect light.

To take maximum advantage of that attribute, we must interpret the *musical* symbols accurately. The composer used a certain language to present the text as *he understood it*; to discover his insights, we must correctly translate that language.

In helping choir members to understand (interpret) the language, we need to impress upon them the value of *all* directions and the necessity of following them closely. This attitude toward the printed page contributes positively in three ways:

1. It makes more careful and thorough readers of the choir members.
2. The musical directions become more meaningful and less a mechanical exercise.
3. You will arrive at a good understanding of the music, and probably do so quickly.

One suggestion is to make up a list of basic musical terms and signs and paste a copy of it in every member's rehearsal folder for quick reference. That could save rehearsal time and teach the "language" as well. Use the terms in rehearsal until they are familiar to all the singers. You will soon equip them with a new vocabulary—painlessly. (Besides, they'll be terribly impressed.)

Notice the phrase "interpreting the musical language accurately." How often have we been guilty of guessing at what the language is saying? Some of us have forgotten what those

Italian words mean (if we ever knew), and we couldn't estimate the speed of a metronomic indication if we saw it going down the street. *No* conductor should be without a good dictionary of musical terms and a metronome; and the less experienced he is, the more often he should use them. He should examine every piece of music for what the musical *language* is saying. (Remember, we've already done that with the text.) Our notational system is evolving into an increasingly specific language, and a careful reading of it will often tell us volumes about what the composer was thinking. *The way to begin any new music is with a literal reading of it.* Here's why:
1. The composer's interpretive suggestions are probably the right (or best) ones.
2. The "right" way to do a piece of music is usually the way we first learned it; this is especially true of tempo.

A musical score (or "chart," as it is appropriately called by pop musicians) is not unlike a roadmap. Most modern ones contain all the signs and directions necessary for an accurate musical journey. *Before* we get involved with "our interpretation," we should carefully consider what the composer has said on the subject. Using the dictionary and metronome, find out what *he* thinks about the tempo, the dynamics, and the style of the piece. That is absolutely fundamental to rehearsal preparation, but it is all too common for directors to strike out blindly through a number with only a cursory and unperceiving glance at the directions so carefully (and lovingly) placed there. An understanding of what the printed page is saying is essential to knowing what the finished product could and should sound like.

All of us have had the experience of hearing someone else perform a number we've been doing for years, and very differently, too. We are shocked at the conductor's insensitivity—only to check the music and discover that he really presented it quite accurately. We usually counter brilliantly by mumbling something about "liking our interpretation much better." What

No conductor should be without a good dictionary of musical terms and a metronome

we mean is that we learned the music without the "handicap" of the directions provided. That treatment has become the correct one to our ear, and any other is wrong, regardless of how closely it may agree with the directions of the composer. Wouldn't it be more reasonable to give the composer's ideas a chance before we impose our own brilliant insight?

Are we ever justified in departing from an exact reading of the music? Of course, and for a variety of good reasons. First, composers and editors are not infallible. Maybe, just maybe, your ideas at this point are better than his (not likely, but maybe, and what I said earlier still goes). Secondly, it's entirely possible that the composer (editor, arranger) only heard the music at the keyboard, which can result in far different conclusions than if he had heard it performed by your Pshaw Chorale. Third, the treatment of a number can, and perhaps should, be varied with the size and ability of the performing group and the acoustical properties of the room involved. For instance, if the group is small and the room large and "dry," that deliberate tempo suggested may simply be impractical, with the music faring much better at a brisker pace.

Of course, if you've trained your singers to read and react to the printed page, you would do well to have a defendable rationale for doing other than the instructions indicate—and there is your teaching opportunity. Discuss it with them. Explain what is on the page, how you intend to depart from it, and why. You can teach them much more than the anthem involved!

Is there a contradiction between the literal approach and the license for liberties? Not at all, and let me summarize.

1. Begin by teaching it like it is.
2. Make any necessary accommodations *after* you have carefully followed the directions—several times.
3. Share the whole interpretive process with the choir members as it unfolds. Make them a part of it and not just a witness to it.

You may feel that the big question remains unanswered: How do you know when to add your own ideas? When can you stop being an Italian-speaking metronome and start being that resourceful, creative genius you know yourself to be?

That is where musicianship rears its beautiful head. It is here that the conductor is separated from the director of traffic. Apply your musical judgment and sensitivity toward the most artistic treatment possible. Then you can know that the resulting interpretation is fair, honest, and artistic.

Music History in Interpretation

The trained musician will already have been exposed to the subject of musical style. Literature that was written in any given period of music history will naturally represent the compositional and performance practice of that period. A knowledge of those practices can be of immeasurable assistance to the director who is teaching "period" music, and of more than passing interest to the choir. Probably a great percentage of the music performed in the average church today was written in this century, and perhaps that is as it should be. A veritable treasure of literature from other times, however, is suitable for our services and manageable by our choirs. The genius and timeless relevance of that music make it as meaningful today as it was when it was written, and our choirs and congregations deserve the opportunity to experience it.

Some of us stay away from period literature simply because we feel inadequate to perform it correctly. Indeed, the subject of historical styles is a broad and involved one. But one doesn't have to be a musicologist in order to bring off a reasonably accurate performance of the music. The great advantage of a considered approach is simply that the music will sound better when performed as the composer intended, and the variety possible can be a fresh breath of air. Even a cursory knowledge of tempo and dynamic practices in the major periods (especially

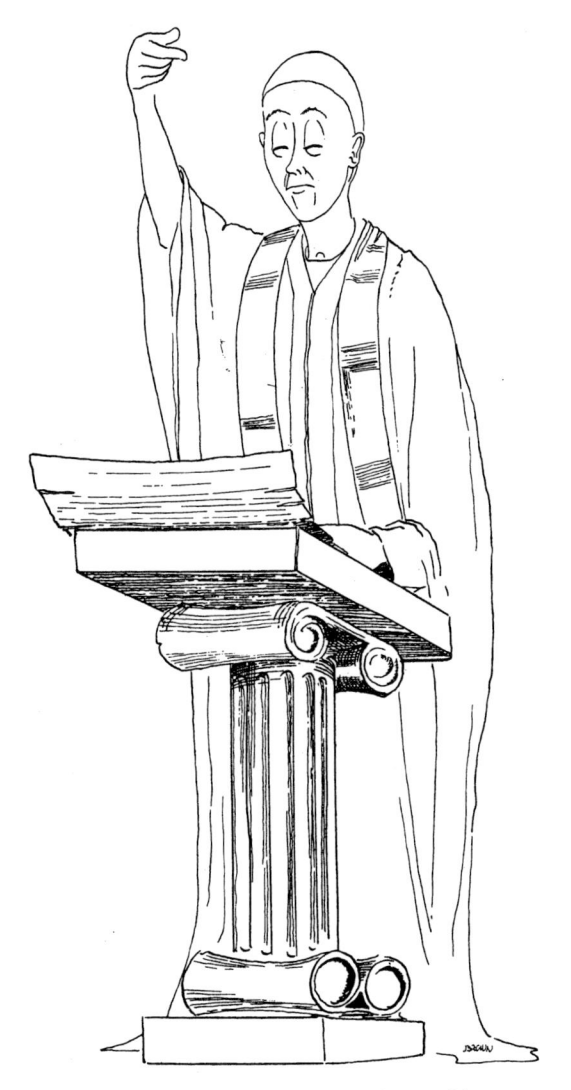

Assistance to the director who is teaching "period" music

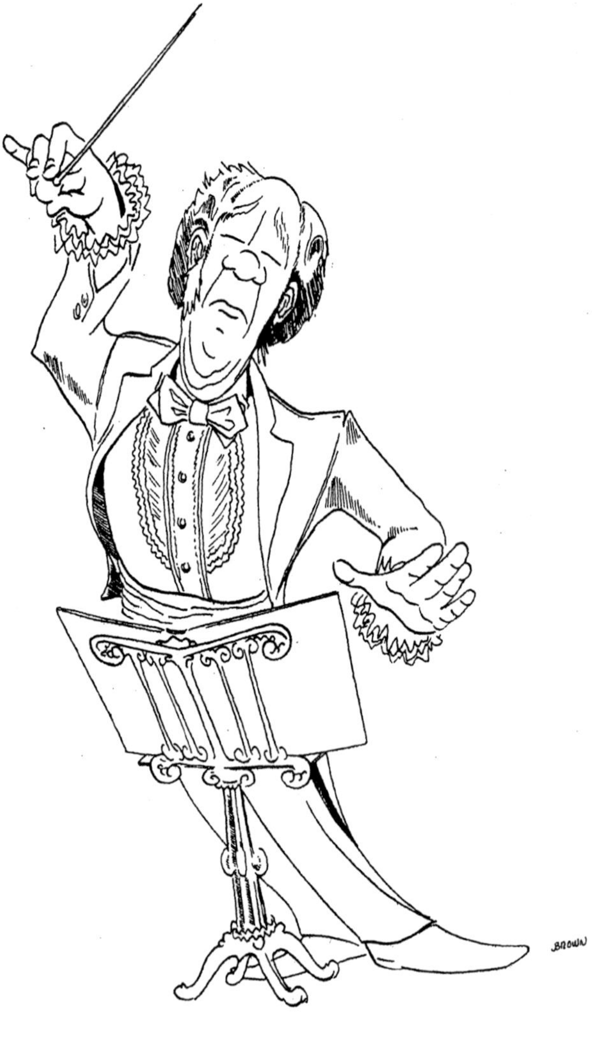
BROWN

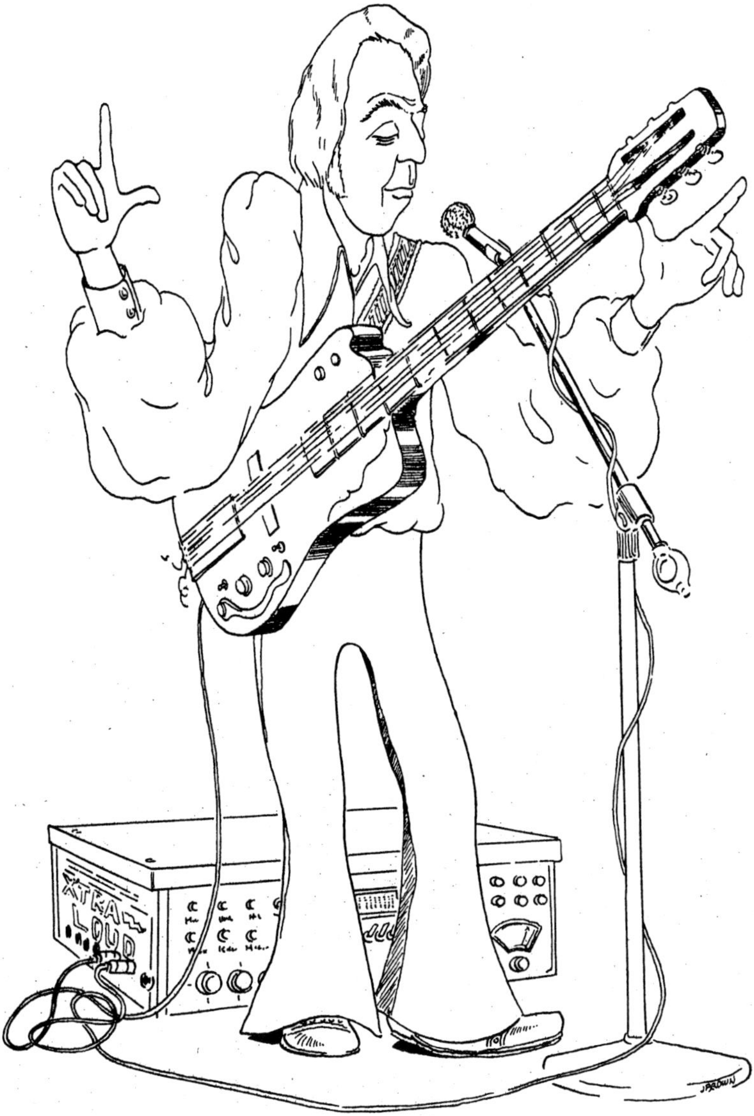
XTRA
LOUD

the Baroque and Romantic) will be a great help in lending style, authenticity, and most importantly, variety to your interpretations. By all means include selected reading in this area as you seek to become an intelligent teacher of interpretation.

Musical Form in Interpretation

Neither time nor the background of our singers permits a detailed discussion of form in music. The alert teacher, however, will overlook no opportunity to weave this important aspect of music into his rehearsals—again not so much as a separate subject, but as a part of the total concept of the music.

An awareness of the way a number is organized seems to be essential to a singer's understanding of what a composer is trying to say through his music. Fortunately, most anthems utilize the more basic, straightforward forms that are easily explained and understood. The most popular is probably ABA; and once it is called to his attention, the singer can become conscious of the symmetry, balance, and structure on which all of the notes are hung. He may be aware for the first time of the calculated use of repetition, which is the basis of musical structure. This common device, repetition, is probably the most direct route for our singers into the land of form. Let's take the ABA anthem and rehearse the two A sections back to back and see what can be learned.

First, it is an efficient way to rehearse. By learning one third of the piece, we are actually dealing with two thirds of the musical material. The matter of different words in the last A part is simple because the notes are already learned. If the harmonization or rhythmic treatment is slightly different, compare and rehearse the differences next to each other in order to avoid stumbling over them later. When the A's are learned, set them aside and concentrate on the "new" material found in B, or, if they please, "the middle part." There may also be opportunity to talk about transitions, modulations, introductions, and codas, all of which will be easily recognizable with little coaching. When the anthem is reassembled, it is not only learned, but learned with a whole new understanding of its structure, logic, and unity. The fact that it is done within context of the rehearsal, and with no special effort to teach form *per se,* is an added bonus.

Another form that serves as an excellent teaching device is the fugue, mainly because there is so much to be learned from it chorally. Begin by teaching the fugal melody to the entire choir, using the most comfortable key. You will have already conserved time and effort. Next, discuss the different treatment by the choir necessary for that melody as opposed to the supportive material that goes with it. Make sure the singers in each section understand when they have it and where it is when they do not. If they are taught always to keep track of the theme, many balance problems will solve themselves. The singer who can hear the theme in another section is not likely singing too loudly himself. That is a valuable lesson that can be transferred to other forms, and contributes to sensitivity to the teamwork so necessary in a good choir.

The approach to music through form can also contribute to its memorization, if that should be one of the goals. An understanding of the structure of music and the use of repetition can shorten that process considerably. From an interpretive point of view, repetition offers a challenge all its own. Good composers almost never repeat anything *verbatim.* Either it is slightly altered physically, or it is to be performed with different nuances. An awareness of this fact can cause a choir member to carefully scrutinize a repeated passage with gratifying results. If the training of knowledgeable, sensitive choir members is our goal, we should by all means introduce them to the architecture of music.

7. The Director as Leader

It is only the people with push
who have a pull.
    THOMAS ROBERT DEWAR, 1864–1930

7. The Director as Leader

IT IS SOMETIMES DIFFICULT for the director to be the firm, assured leader that he needs to be. That is frequently the case when he is a part-time or volunteer director whose primary training may be in an entirely different field. Or perhaps he is young and faced with the prospect of telling his elders what to do. Maybe he is a "she," who is uncomfortable in this aggressive role in the presence of the men in the choir. Even if he is a well-trained, professional, middle-aged male, he may still have problems taking control. Let's talk about that.

It is imperative that the choir director be the leader. It's not just a matter of superior knowledge on the subject, though hopefully that would be the case. It's certainly not a question of arrogance, for few of us believe in our own infallibility. It just goes with the job. When we agree to serve as director, we are assuming the responsibility for making the decisions, musical and otherwise, that pertain thereto. A choir in rehearsal is not a democratic organization where all opinions are aired and voted upon. It is a dictatorship, albeit a thoughtful, considerate,

... a dictatorship, albeit a benevolent one

benevolent one. Apart from the rehearsal, we can and should seek all the counsel available for whatever our needs are. In rehearsal, we are the final arbiter, and must make decisions that face us, quickly and unapologetically, *even if we are wrong.* If you ever doubt that nature abhors a vacuum, just abdicate that responsibility for a few minutes and see what happens. In thirty seconds there will be more suggestions, opinions, and alternatives than you could use in a month. Some of them might even be good, but the rehearsal will be in rudderless disarray.

The shy among us must realize that there is no oversized ego or arrogance implied in assuming the role of leader. This is simply the name of the game. To perform our duties adequately, we must discharge those responsibilities with as much grace, humility, and *firmness* as we can muster. If you are the leader, be leader. Otherwise, sing in the choir.

The Director as Disciplinarian

Closely related to the role as leader is the role of disciplinarian. The problems are a bit different (and surprisingly similar) between Youth and Adult choirs, but the outcome must always be the same, and never in doubt. The director must maintain an orderly, disciplined rehearsal.

Of all the failings common to choir directors everywhere, the failure to maintain discipline must be the most common of all, and certainly one of the most difficult to surmount. If we are going to accomplish anything creative and artistic in our rehearsals, it will be out of an atmosphere of discipline and order, not of chaos. We can be the epitome of charm, grace, wit, and musicianship; but if we cannot hold an orderly rehearsal, we are doomed to failure. Teaching music to adults and youth, or to senior citizens or preschoolers, is predicated on the assumption that an orderly environment is present.

Poor disciplinarians usually develop as the result of one or both of these assumptions: (1) It is presumptuous for one to

The director's role as disciplinarian

demand the attention of the group (especially adults); and (2) one will be better liked if he is easygoing and "one of the guys" (a common attitude in dealing with Youth choirs). The irony is that the opposite is the case. Our stock as director *and* person rises or falls with our ability to maintain discipline in a pleasant, inoffensive, but firm manner. It is paradoxical but true that choir members, old and young, will create all kinds of havoc in rehearsal, then go away grumbling because the director permitted it to happen! Let's look at what is involved in maintaining good discipline and try to determine how we can best fulfil this part of our responsibility as teachers.

The key to good discipline, whether it be as parents or choir directors, can be summed up in three words: firmness, fairness, and consistency. The ground rules for rehearsals must be clearly spelled out and then firmly enforced. Corrections or rebukes should be immediate and in proportion to the "crime." A harsh scolding for a minor infraction is both unfair and morale destroying.

Consistency is perhaps the most desirable and difficult virtue of all, and is essential to fairness. If we tolerate certain forms of behavior on one day and then react strongly against them on another, we have been both inconsistent and unfair. Choir members deserve to know what is expected of them and what they can expect from us.

The most common forms of disorder in most rehearsals are talking and inattention. Before we sentence our choir members, we need to take a little personal inventory. The choir members frequently talk too much because the director talks too much. We may become enamored of the sound of our own voices and the wisdom of our words, while the choir members are just becoming bored. If they are not kept busy singing, they usually get busy talking, so maybe their gregariousness is caused by our lengthy discourses.

One of the most distracting disturbances is that low undercurrent of conversation that often begins the moment the choir stops singing. It's especially difficult to deal with because it has no focal point; there is no definite place to take hold of the problem. The biggest mistake we can make here is to attempt to rise above the hubbub and go on with the rehearsal. To do this is to forfeit our role as leader and enter into a competition with the choir members for the floor. The more they talk, the higher we raise our voices; and the louder we get, the noisier they become, and so on *ad infinitum*. How much more effective it is to simply stop (in midsentence, if necessary) and wait quietly for the gabfest to subside. To look at those in the offending group, if they are localized, will usually hasten the restoration of order; and it calls the attention of all choir members to the problem area without your saying a word. When the disturbers realize that you (and the rest of the choir) have been sitting there patiently (?) waiting for them to conclude their conversation, your point has been made. If they appear to be nonchalant about it, an appropriate comment from you is in order. The important thing is to assume your right to their attention. Do not attempt to rehearse until you have it.

A similar kind of disorder occurs when choir members attempt to do their own rehearsing. The director stops to make a correction, and seven mini-rehearsals materialize throughout the choir. Their motives are pure, their objectives commendable, and their zeal praiseworthy, but the noise is just as destructive. It may seem inefficient to them, but in the long run, time is saved and the music served when problems are solved, notes are corrected, and questions answered from the podium, and not from within the membership of the choir. Once the singers understand that you prefer not to have this kind of "help" from them, rehearsal discipline should improve.

Contrast those kinds of disturbances with the occasional wisecrack from the wags on the back row. I consider these not only unobjectionable but welcome, if the timing is right. The important thing is that it be shared by the whole choir and not by two or three sitting together. A good laugh can *momentarily* relax the group and enhance the spirit of fellowship so vital to a choir. Just be certain that the break in concentration is only momentary and that all go quickly back to work.

If we were to call attention to another attribute of the effective disciplinarian, it would be good humor. The firmest rebuke can be softened and made palatable if the tone is light, or the point humorously made. Biting sarcasm or ego-deflating jibes may make us feel clever or vindicated, but that is taking unfair advantage of our singers. Beyond that, they are basically unchristian and have no place in the kind of organization we want to have.

The best disciplinarians I know are people of immense self-control. They maintain their emotional equilibrium in all situations and against all provocations. The screaming tyrant may have a certain dubious glamor when viewed from a safe distance; but, again, this kind of behavior is inconsistent with what we believe should characterize our relationship with others. It is imperative that our little monarchy is presided over with patience, good humor, and respect for our "subjects." It is a humbling thought, especially for the professional director, to realize that most of the people in our Adult choirs know more about our profession than we know about theirs. In other words, they are able to function very creditably as amateur musicians, where you or I would be a one-man holocaust as an amateur druggist, electrician, or cook. The Christian dimension aside, these dear people are deserving of our love and respect, and should be disciplined accordingly.

But disciplined they must be, and it is the director's job to do it. He may be literally overflowing with wonderful things to teach his choir members, but the most brilliant teacher is ineffective until he has the attention of his students.

8. The Director as Teacher to the Congregation

Once men sang together round a table in chorus; now one man sings alone for the absurd reason that he can sing better.

G. K. Chesterton, 1874–1936

8. The Director as Teacher to the Congregation

THUS FAR our discussion has been limited to groups that are formally and regularly involved in rehearsal, or instructional conditions. But what of the congregation, the body that we are so fond of referring to as our "largest choir"? What is our responsibility and opportunity as teachers to them? I suggest it is considerable. The material to be taught will naturally center around the music sung by the congregation Sunday by Sunday. Even the congregation that boasts a wide repertoire of hymns is likely to be appallingly ignorant about the hymns they sing—and probably love. Many of our hymns are no longer relevant to the contemporary congregation, but most all of them would be considerably more meaningful if the worshiper knew something about their birth. Both the use of relevant hymns and the necessity for greater insight into what we are singing create a rich opportunity for the director-teacher.

There will be no effort more appreciated by our congregations than that expended in behalf of the "good old hymns." While you and I may be lukewarm toward some of them, there will undoubtedly be people whose entire attitude toward you and the music program will be shaped by your attention, or lack of it, to this one area. More importantly, a bit of teaching in the song services can provoke new, and revitalize dormant, interest in many old and frayed favorites. While I believe it is fair to say that some of our favorite hymns are no longer relevant, we must also admit that much of the problem lies in our lack of awareness of what the writer was trying to say, *and why*.

Perhaps I can illustrate one possible approach to teaching the congregation about hymns through the work of one man. For example, to fully understand the hymns of Isaac Watts, our people need to know something of his background, his theology, and his philosophy of hymns. By sharing only a few brief facts about the man, we can understand things about his hymns that we've never seen before. To wit:

Watts lived from 1674 to 1748 in England. He was a Calvinist by theology. Among other things, that meant that his early exposure was to hymns of the metrical-psalm type. Calvin believed that only the "inspired words of God" (Bible) were fit for worship, and therefore limited his followers to the singing of Scriptures, mostly psalms, that had been adjusted to conform to a regular meter. By the time Watts was a young man, that initially fervent, vigorous singing had deteriorated badly, and Watts felt that some changes were in order. That attitude and three important points will serve well in understanding his hymns today.

1. In the matter of construction, Watts departed from Calvin's belief regarding the exclusive use of Scriptures. He believed that if one was to praise God in song, then the song should be his own, and not the words of another far removed in time and geography. As a result, he wrote what were called hymns of "human composure" in contrast to those which utilized only the "words of God." He set them to easy meters and used whatever tunes were at hand. (Could some of them have

been "secular"?) While not expressing himself very subtly, he certainly made his intentions clear when he said his purpose was "to write down to the level of vulgar capacities, and to furnish hymns for the meanest [lowliest] of Christians." He succeeded admirably, and his hymns of "human composure" were happily and gratefully sung by those for whom he had written them.

2. Watts was not opposed to the metrical psalms, but felt that any that were used should be overhauled to reflect the language and experiences of the worshipers. So he bent himself to the task of rewriting the psalms in such a manner that the "meanest of Christians" could understand them and sing them sympathetically. Watts did not attempt to translate or even paraphrase the psalmist, but rather to imitate him. Consequently, his efforts represented a blend of David and Watts with some noteworthy results.

Again, the overriding consideration in the mind of Watts was the use of a language and style that his people could understand. He published a collection of his "imitations" that he called *The Psalms of David Imitated in the Language of the New Testament, and Applied to the Christian State and Worship*. In the preface he cheerfully made his case:

"I could never persuade myself that the best Way to raise a devout Frame in plain Christians was to bring a King or a Captain into their Churches and let him lead and dictate the Worship in his own Style of Royalty, or in the Language of a Field of Battle. Does every menial Servant in the Assembly know how to use these words devoutly—'A Bow of Steel is broken in mine Arms,' Ps. 18:34. Would I encourage a Parish-Clerk to stand up in the midst of a County Church, and bid all the People joyn with his Words and say, 'I will praise thee upon a Psaltery; or, I will open my dark Saying upon the Harp . . .' Why must all that will sing a Psalm at Church use such words as if they were to play upon Harp or Psaltery, when Thousands never saw such an Instrument? Have not your Spirits taken Wing and mounted up near to God and Glory with the Song of David on your Tongue? But on a sudden the Clerk has proposed the next line to your Lips with . . . Burnt-Offering or Hyssop, with New-Moons and Trumpets and Tumbrils in it, with Confessions of Sins which you never committed, cursing such Enemies as you never had, giving Thanks for such Victories as you never obtained . . . How have all your Souls been discomposed at once, and the Strings of Harmony all untuned!"

3. Although Watts disagreed with Calvin on the use of hymns of "human composure," his theology was Calvinist through and through. Basically, this meant that he was rigidly, even harshly, fundamentalist and predestinationalist, with little concern for the social ills around him, and none whatever for a lost world. If God intended for a man to be saved, then God would save him, and without the necessity for human interference. Watts's hymns faithfully reflected this theology, and many of them were grim and foreboding indeed. Happily, the worst have been culled from the hymnals over the years, and the more unpalatable of his dogmas are laid to rest. Nevertheless, his attitudes are naturally present in varying and subtle degrees. Now take a new look at his hymns.

Armed with this kind of information, the director and his people can sing "When I Survey the Wondrous Cross" or "We're Marching to Zion" with an intelligent appreciation for the fact that these are hymns of "human composure," and represented a radical and courageous departure from the *status quo*. They can sing with hymnal and Bible open together and realize, perhaps for the first time, that "Jesus Shall Reign Where'er the Sun" is Psalm 72 imitated, and "O God, Our Help in Ages Past" is Psalm 90 revisited. They can sing "When I can read my title clear To mansions in the skies"—and understand Watts's Calvinistic caution in claiming to be one of God's elect with any degree of certainty.

This thumbnail sketch of the Reverend Dr. Watts and his

hymns is simply an attempt to illustrate how much more meaningful even familiar hymns can be with just a modest amount of background information. The information is readily available from a variety of sources and can be shared with a congregation in interesting and brief presentations. How refreshing our hymn introductions can become if we sprinkle them with relevant facts about what we are singing. It will require some preparation on our part, but we can't expect to teach what we ourselves haven't absorbed.

A related opportunity to teach is found in material described as "new." Our congregations tend to use this adjective to describe any hymn that is unknown to them, whether it is three weeks old or three centuries old. If the "new" hymn is old, it needs to be presented as intelligently (background) and attractively as possible. As in the case of the Watts illustration, attempt to sketch the personality and/or circumstances that helped create the hymn. A hymn is never born in a vacuum. Make its message live for your people. If you find that impossible, forget the hymn, regardless of how much *you* like it. This brings us to the second teaching opportunity and some soul-searching on the part of the director. What is the role of the "new" sound in church music? How can it be reconciled with the old, and how can we help our people at this point?

A great deal is being said these days about the need for updating our church music. Young people are increasingly vocal about the "dated" anthems and "old" hymns that they contend are virtually meaningless. More and more they are responding to sacred or semi-sacred texts sung to popular tunes and rhythms. "This is our language," the teen-agers say.

They have a point. The good news may be centuries old, but we must be certain that it is expressed in a language appropriate for our time. Nowhere is the generation gap more noticeable than in the hymns we sing.

Nearly every hymn in the hymnal was born out of a particular need and speaks to a specific point. A hymn written in seventeenth-century England naturally uses seventeenth-century English, and addresses itself to the theological or social issues of that day. For many of us, however, the issues that inspired much of our hymnody have long since become obscure, leaving us with unfamiliar language, set to the music of another age.

Bible translators have recognized the need for presenting the Scriptures in contemporary language. There are several editions written in modern, almost conversational, English. Yet, every Sunday we trudge through poetry that speaks of Ebenezers, sheep, hosannas, rods and staffs, swords and bucklers, etc. Did this poetry once speak clearly and forcibly? Of course. Does it now? It is doubtful. Then why are these hymns still so much a part of our worship services?

1. These hymns have proved themselves worthy because they have endured. Time has a way of sifting out the dross and leaving only the gold (to borrow a phrase from the hymnal). In other words, these "old" hymns obviously contain poetry of exceptional merit, or they would simply die of mediocrity. Stilted to twentieth-century ears or not, these hymns still have the power to communicate.

2. We all tend to love the hymns that we learned in our formative years. Perhaps we understand them; perhaps we do not. Maybe they are presently relevant; maybe they are not. The point is—to us, those are the "good old hymns." They make us feel comfortable and secure. We sing them mechanically—and sometimes meaninglessly—completely unaware of, or unconcerned about, the strange symbolism. The same handful of hymns is sung by generation after generation, not because they speak to the needs of the day (which they may), and probably not because of their literary merit (which may be considerable), but because they are comfortable and undemanding. There is only one small catch. It is virtually impossible to

achieve unanimity on just which hymns *are* the "good old hymns." That depends on the age, as well as the regional, social, and economic background of the individual. A good old hymn for one group may be new and not especially good to another. We are really talking about the hymns we have known since childhood.

3. There seems to be a dearth of fresh, newly written hymns. I wonder why. God is surely still speaking, revealing, and inspiring. Yet, our preachers and poets, not to mention the largest body of professionally trained church musicians history has known, are failing to add appreciably to a grand, but antiquated, body of hymnody. If that is the case, perhaps there just is not a big enough market for them. How sad that in an age of exploration and nuclear fission, riots, and assassinations, we are content to review weekly the rhymed perils of John Wesley and the versified theology of Isaac Watts.

There are dozens of publishers cranking out choir music by the bale. There is certainly nothing wrong with that market. Do you suppose the situation could be another indication of the spectator syndrome? It is all right for the choir to sing a new anthem so long as it's not *too* different. But the music director takes his life (or job) in his hands if he tampers very much with the hymn singing.

But tamper we must if we expect to minister adequately to all ages and experiences. We can make ourselves aware of current efforts to broaden and update our hymnody. There are some people already deeply involved in doing just that. The Hymn Society of America is doing much to encourage the writing and publishing of new hymns and tunes. The Church Music Department of the Sunday School Board of the Southern Baptist Convention periodically sponsors a hymn writing competition, which has already made available some exciting contemporary hymns. Inform yourself. Inform the congregation. Share with them that changeless gospel in an ever changing medium.

9. Continuing Preparation

The gent who wakes up and finds himself a success hasn't been asleep.
     WILSON MIZNER, 1876–1933

9. Continuing Preparation

ANY MUSIC DIRECTOR worth his salt has a desire to know more than he does and to be better than he is. In this technical and rapidly changing field of church music, it behooves all of us to constantly freshen and update our knowledge and skills. The music degree is really a license to begin to learn, not a terminal point in one's education; and the nonprofessional director has a whole world of discovery before him. Consider for a moment the possibilities available to nearly all of us for professional improvement.

The most obvious training available is formal schooling. If there is a college or university in your town, it will undoubtedly offer courses that provide or refresh backgrounds in a wide range of pertinent subjects. Schedules can usually be arranged to allow you to take a few hours per semester. If no school is available, then a private teacher can be an excellent source of instruction and skill development. Private study not only enhances your own performance capabilities, but it also increases the skills you bring to your own "classroom."

Another avenue to self-improvement is through music workshops or clinics. Our seminaries and colleges sponsor them annually. State and associational music leaders periodically provide them; and the music weeks at Ridgecrest and Glorieta are without peer in the breadth, depth, and caliber of experiences made available. I've known several men and women who, without a minute of formal musical training, have acquired substantial musical background simply by availing themselves of the frequent opportunities to participate in these kinds of training. Some clinics feature the finest teachers and conductors to be found, and they will cost anywhere from nothing to a few dollars!

A third way to assure continued musical growth is a bit more subtle, often unrecognized, and consequently frequently ignored. That is the growth that comes almost automatically through experiencing new repertoire. There is no better exercise for musical muscles than pitting them against new and (hopefully) increasingly sophisticated musical problems.

All of us know people who trot out the same threadbare handful of choral numbers and cantatas year after year. This practice deprives the choir, congregation, and director of a varied diet and results in stunted musical growth. I believe this to be true especially in the area of oratorios and cantatas that offer unusually rich opportunities for the musicians to grow. No work, regardless of its individual merit, is worth doing year after year to the exclusion of other equally valuable scores. It is easy and comfortable to remount the same old war-horses. It is difficult and time consuming to search out and master works that are new to you. In the long run, however, it is one of the most pleasant and rewarding methods of insuring a measure of continued musical growth.

Personal Learning Activities

CHAPTER 1
1. What is meant by "long-range" planning?
2. What factors must be considered in establishing quarterly rehearsal and performance schedules?
3. How many numbers should be scheduled for a one-hour rehearsal?
4. What are *bonus* rehearsals?
5. When should *bonus* rehearsals be scheduled?

CHAPTER 2
1. List the three primary areas of rehearsal priorities.
2. How are priorities established?
3. How can you sum up, in one statement, the essence of establishing priorities?

CHAPTER 3
1. What are two advantages of diaphragmatic breathing?
2. Why is the *staccato* exercise good for learning correct breath application?
3. What can loud singing be compared to?

CHAPTER 4
1. What are the two basic decisions a conductor must make in his approach to vowels?
2. What is "vowel color"?
3. Is there a difference in teaching vowels to Adults and Youth choir members?
4. Generally speaking, how strong should consonants be?
5. What are voiced and unvoiced consonants?
6. How can seating arrangement affect blend?

CHAPTER 5
1. Should the director teach conducting to his choir members?
2. What three things should the preparation beat indicate?

3. What is the *ictus*?
4. What determines the strength of the release?
5. What is a cue?
6. What are the three "watchdogs" of conducting?
7. What are the disadvantages of singing with the choir while conducting?
8. What is meant by "negating the beat"?
9. What special problems present themselves when conducting instrumentalists?
10. Why is the cue particularly important to the instrumentalist?

CHAPTER 6
1. What is the twofold approach to interpreting choral music?
2. Why should the choir members learn to interpret all directions in the score?
3. How should we begin to teach new music?
4. Are we ever justified in departing from an exact reading of the music? Why?
5. How can we use music history in interpretation?
6. What should we teach the choir member about form?

CHAPTER 7
1. What factors tend to keep a director from being a disciplinarian?
2. What three words sum up the key to good discipline?
3. What is the most desirable virtue of the disciplinarian?

CHAPTER 8
1. Do we have a responsibility to teach the congregation?
2. What were Watts's main contributions to hymnody?
3. Name two hymns written by Watts.
4. Why do we still use "old" hymns?
5. Why do we need new hymns?
6. What are two sources of new hymns?

CHAPTER 9
1. Why should the director continue his education, even informally?
2. What are three ways that a director may continue to grow musically?